THE
BABE
BOOK

Other books by Ernestine G. Miller

The Sportswomen's Daybook
The Art of Advertising

THE BABE BOOK

Baseball's Greatest Legend Remembered

Ernestine Gichner Miller

Foreword by Julia Ruth Stevens

Andrews McMeel
Publishing

Kansas City

00 01 02 03 04 TWP 10 9 8 7 6 5 4 3 2 1

Library of Congress Cataloging-in-Publication Data
Miller, Ernestine G.
   The Babe book : baseball's greatest legend remembered / Ernestine Miller;
foreword by Julia Ruth Stevens.
      p. cm.
   ISBN 0-7407-1012-5
      1. Ruth, Babe, 1895-1948—Anecdotes. 2. Baseball players—United States—
Biography. I. Title.

GV865.R8 M54 2000
796.357'092—dc21
[B]   00-29945

Book design by Holly Camerlinck

All photographs printed courtesy of The Babe Ruth Birthplace Museum,
Baltimore, Maryland

To

Michael Gibbons, Director,
Greg Schwalenberg, Curator,
The Staff and Board of Directors of
The Babe Ruth Birthplace and Oriole Museum,
Baltimore, Maryland.

In memory of my mother, Gertrude Gichner, who took me
as a young girl to Washington Senators games and taught
me about baseball, and in memory of my father, Lawrence
Gichner, who inspired my love for history.

To my daughter, Helene Stephanie Miller.

Contents

FOREWORD

My father, Babe Ruth, was the unanimous choice of America's sports organizations as the greatest baseball player of the century. It was truly my pleasure to have been part of the many awards and tributes he received. Now, as another century of baseball is under way, we get this fresh look at his legacy in *The Babe Book*.

This wonderful array of engaging quotes—many from people who knew him—captures his life and career from virtually every angle. Fans of all ages can feel the force of his swing, share his fun-loving personality, and be moved by his genuine love for children.

The close to ninety photographs come from the collection of The Babe Ruth Birthplace and Orioles Museum in Baltimore and show his life in ways words alone could never conjure. Many of the photos are published here for the first time.

I urge you to visit the historic Babe Ruth Birthplace, located just two blocks from Oriole Park at Camden Yards. It serves as a daily celebration of Daddy's lasting contribution to our national pastime, the greatest game ever invented!

Here's to enjoying *The Babe Book*.

Sincerely,

Julia Ruth Stevens

Julia Ruth Stevens

ACKNOWLEDGMENTS

With grateful appreciation to Carrie Potter for her assistance throughout the project.

A very special thank-you to Greg Schwalenberg for his valuable help in selecting the photographs.

Morton Mindell, Baltimore, Maryland—a true baseball aficionado.

Julia Ruth Stevens for her continued devotion and support of The Babe Ruth Birthplace Museum.

All black-and-white photographs are from the archives of The Babe Ruth Birthplace Museum. Color photographs are by Jeff Goldman, Baltimore, Maryland.

THE
BABE

George Herman Ruth

February 6, 1895
Baltimore, Maryland

August 16, 1948
New York, New York

Babe Ruth

INTRODUCTION

"If you weren't around in those times, I don't think you could appreciate what a figure the Babe was. He was bigger than the President."

—RICHARDS VIDNER, *sportswriter for the* New York Times, *quoted in*
Jerome Holtzman, The Armchair Book of Baseball

The Babe went from a poor, incorrigible youth, raised from age seven at St. Mary's Industrial School for Boys in Baltimore, to the quintessential American sports figure. His story is of a man who understood and then mastered his athleticism. By the early age of twenty-one, he had transformed himself into America's most compelling hero, filling stadiums around the country with adoring fans. Soon his persona extended beyond baseball—everyone knew Babe Ruth.

Often called the Bambino and the Sultan of Swat, Babe mesmerized the nation for over twenty-one years with his unmatched muscle, booming bat, and gregarious personality. His towering home runs brought a sense of high drama to baseball that the game had never known.

When Babe joined the Boston Red Sox in 1914 at age nineteen, it was as a

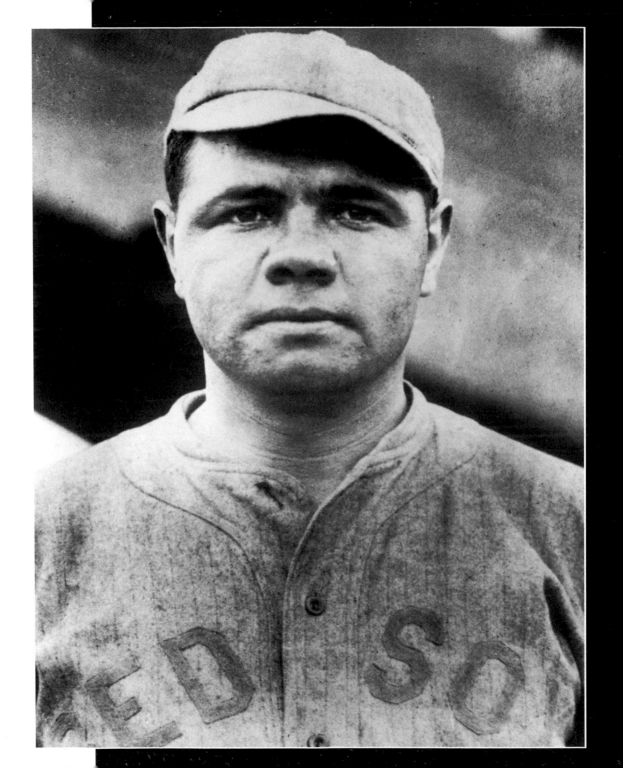

pitcher. Baseball statistics reported on in newspapers included batting averages, sacrifices, and stolen bases—not home runs. The Bambino came along and changed that. In 1919 he hit twenty-nine home runs and in December was sold by Boston owner Harry Frazee to the Yankees for $125,000. In 1920 Babe, now age twenty-five and playing left field full-time, hit fifty-four home runs—more than any other American League team that year, except the Yankees. He also produced a slugging percentage of .847, a record that has yet to be matched. He hit fifty-nine home runs in 1921 and was firmly in place as baseball's superstar. On September 30, 1927, the Babe slugged his historic six-tieth and set a single-season record that remained a milestone for thirty-four years until Roger Maris broke it in 1961 with sixty-one. In total, Babe set fifty-six major league records and 192 American League records, many of which still stand today.

With his power, intense concentration, confidence, and unsurpassed devotion, he was the very fabric of baseball. In 1998, perhaps the greatest "home run year" of all, with Mark McGwire's seventy and Sammy Sosa's sixty-six, Babe's presence was still very much alive. He was at the top of every "All–Century List," and when the next century of greats is recognized the one constant in sports who should endure the test of time is Babe Ruth. He will be enshrined forever as the folk hero of baseball, like a national heirloom passed down from one generation to the next. Today, more than sixty-six years since he last played the game, the world continues to celebrate what he left us . . . It all goes back to the Babe.

A legendary pitcher for the Boston Red Sox, 1914–19

If Babe had not existed, it would have been impossible to invent him. He not only changed the rules, equipment, and strategy of baseball but he changed and shaped the role of athletes in society as the first superstar of sports. Between his revolutionary long ball hitting and his involvement with the media, he revitalized baseball and became a hero to many Americans.

Always an impeccable dresser, Babe is shown here holding his "signature" camel hair top-coat and wearing the matching cap.

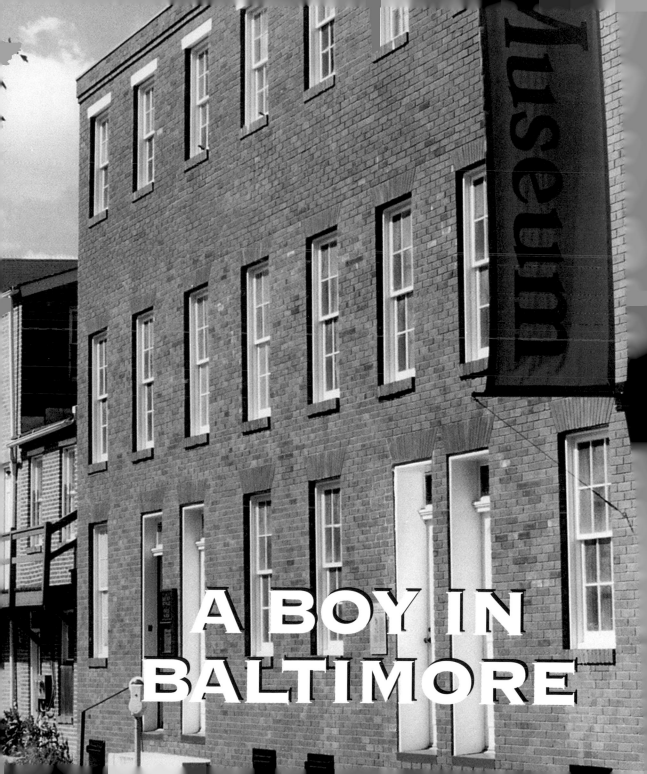

A BOY IN
BALTIMORE

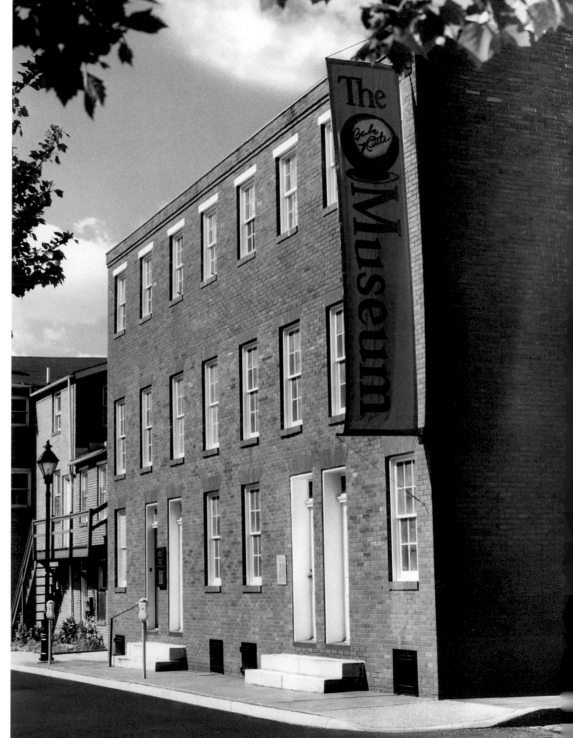

Babe Ruth was born in this row house (third door from right) at 216 Emory Street, Baltimore, Maryland, on February 6, 1895. Today these four residences house The Babe Ruth Birthplace Museum, where treasured artifacts and memorabilia are on exhibit.

> **"He was a waif on the Baltimore waterfront at the turn of the century. The chances of him becoming world famous were about the odds of winning the lottery."**
>
> —MICHAEL GIBBONS, *executive director of The Babe Ruth Birthplace Museum, Baltimore*

As a young boy, George Herman Ruth was unruly and hard for his parents to handle. At age seven he was sent to St. Mary's Industrial School for Boys at a cost to his parents of $15 a month. The school was home to eight hundred boys from broken homes, poor families, and those who were delinquent and incorrigible, ranging in age from five to twenty-one. George was listed as an incorrigible. He studied vocational subjects, tailoring, and shirtmaking.

Occasionally George came home, but he always returned to the care of the Xaverian Brothers who ran the school. His mother Kate died when he was thirteen and his father, who earned a living as a saloon keeper, died in 1918 when George was twenty-three.

George was a natural athlete and loved baseball. His skills were mostly developed from hours of practice with his mentor, Brother Matthias, a tall, athletic man. At first George was a left-handed catcher using a right-handed mitt, but after playing every position, he settled as a pitcher and became the star of the team. On February 27, 1914, he left the confines of St. Mary's to join the Baltimore Orioles for $25 a week. He was nineteen years old and, at six feet two inches tall bigger than other players. Jack Dunn, the owner of the Orioles (a minor league team in those days), became his legal guardian.

George had limited awareness of the world outside of St. Mary's and lacked manners and maturity, but he had a single ambition . . . to use his power, courage, and tenacity to become a major league baseball player.

"I chewed tobacco when I was seven, not that I enjoyed it—but from my observation around the saloon—it seemed the normal thing to do."

—BABE RUTH, *as told to Bob Considine,* The Babe Ruth Story, *1948*

On the ball field at St. Mary's Industrial School for Boys (1911). Today it is Cardinal Gibbons High School.

"I probably was a victim of circumstances. I spent most of the first seven years of my life living over my father's saloon at 426 West Camden Street in Baltimore. When I wasn't living over it, I was living in it, studying the rough talk of the longshoremen, merchant sailors, roustabouts, and water-front bums. When I wasn't living in it I was living in the neighborhood streets. I had a rotten start and it took me a long time to get my bearings."

—BABE RUTH, *as told to Bob Considine*, The Babe Ruth Story, *1948*

George's natural ability was apparent at an early age. By the time he was eight or nine he was playing with the twelve-year-old team, when he was twelve he was competing with the sixteen-year-old team, and at the age of sixteen he was on the varsity. "I could always hit," Ruth said in later years, "but it was Brother Matthias who made me a fielder."

—LAWRENCE S. RITTER AND MARK RUCKER, The Babe:
The Game That Ruth Built, *1997*

None of the teams facing Big George, either from within the school or from the outside, could stand up against his pitching. He rarely fanned less than a dozen a game.

—TOM MEANY, Babe Ruth: The Big Moments
and the Big Fella, *1947*

Babe holding his catcher's mitt and mask outside St. Mary's
Industrial School for Boys circa 1913

Babe (second row, far left) with his teammates at St. Mary's.
He was the catcher on the championship team and proudly
displays his mitt and mask.

No one ever had told him that left-handed catchers were unfashionable, not to say obsolete and it never occurred to him that they might be. He was bigger than most of the kids and stronger than any of them and he liked to catch. He had a great arm and few kids stole any bases on him.

There was a mild inconvenience, of course. The only catcher's mitt the team boasted was for a right-handed boy, so the Babe had to flip it off every time he made a throw to second base. Still, one couldn't be choosey.

There came a day when the other kids discovered the Babe could pitch with greater speed and control and cunning than any one else. Forthwith, he became a pitcher. It was the contention of the other kids that anybody could catch but that only he could pitch. This was all right with the Babe. So it happened that he left the shelter of St. Mary's and entered the outside world as a pitcher and not as a catcher—and he found that he could go very far indeed.

—FRANK GRAHAM, *sportswriter,* New York Sun, *from the 1920s to 1940s*

"It was at St. Mary's that I met and learned to love the greatest man I've ever known. His name was Brother Matthias. He was the father I needed. He taught me to read and write—and he taught me the difference between right and wrong.

"It was Brother Matthias who finally struck upon the thing to hold my interest and keep me happy. It was baseball. Once I had been introduced to school athletics I was satisfied and happy. Even as a kid I was big for my age, and because of my size I used to get most any job I liked on the team. Sometimes I pitched. Sometimes I caught, and frequently I played in the outfield and infield. It was all the same to me. All I wanted was to play. I didn't care where."

—BABE RUTH, *quoted in* The Baseball Anthology, *edited by Joseph Wallace, 1994*

Brother Matthias spent a disproportionate amount of time with the youngster, considering that about eight hundred others were also in his custody. He helped him with his schoolwork, talked with him about his future, and was always ready with support and encouragement.

He also played a critical role in developing and shaping young George Ruth's God-given raw baseball talent. He taught by practice and by repetition: by hitting baseballs to Ruth and others for hour after hour.

—LAWRENCE S. RITTER AND MARK RUCKER, The Babe: The Game That Ruth Built, *1997*

◆　◆　◆

Every boy at St. Mary's received proper schooling while at the same time he was given a certain kind of work to do. The Babe had a job in the shirt factory, where he made work shirts for an outside firm. The money earned was entered in a book to the boy's account. Then each evening after supper there was a little store that opened for about an hour, from which could be obtained such things as candy, cakes, peanuts and other such stuff.

Each evening when the store opened Babe would buy a hat full of mixed candies and pass them around to the orphan boys who had no parents or friends.

I shall never forget him because at that time I happened to be one of those unfortunate boys and for over two years the only candy I ever received was from the Babe.

—LOU LEISMAN, *schoolmate, quoted in the pamphlet* "I Was with Babe Ruth at St. Mary's"

Babe (second row, third from left) was a star catcher before becoming a pitcher on the St. Mary's team.

"I look back on St. Mary's as one of the most constructive periods of my life. I'm as proud of it as any Harvard man is of his school."

—BABE RUTH, *as told to Bob Considine,* The Babe Ruth Story, *1948*

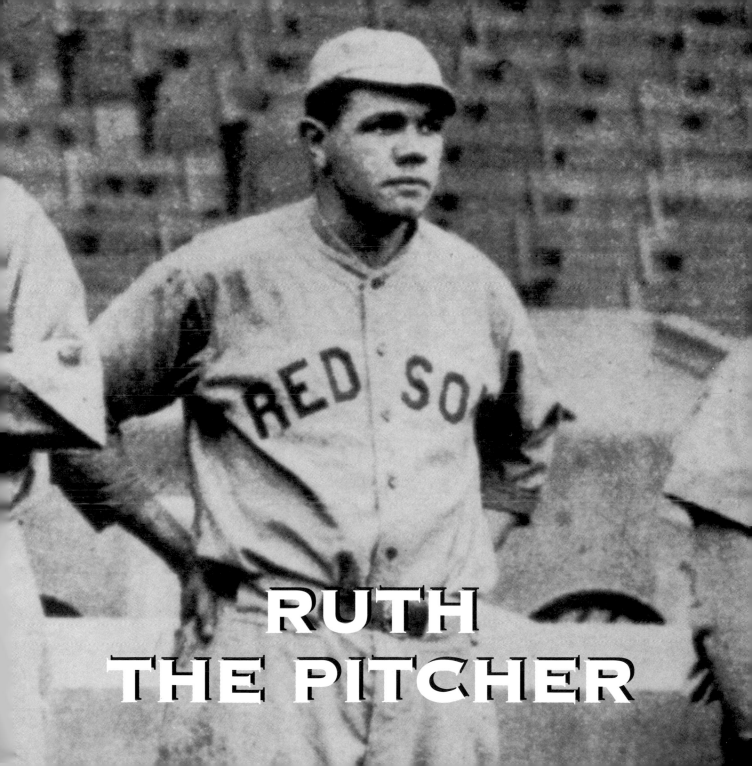

RUTH
THE PITCHER

"You know, I saw it happen, from beginning to end. But sometimes I still can't believe what I saw: this nineteen-year-old kid, crude, poorly educated, only lightly brushed by the social veneer we call civilization, gradually transformed into the idol of American youth and the symbol of baseball the world over—a man loved by more people and with an intensity of feeling that perhaps has never been equaled before or since. I saw a man transformed from a human being into something pretty close to a god."

—HARRY HOOPER, *Boston Red Sox teammate and right fielder, 1917, quoted in Lawrence S. Ritter,* The Glory of Their Times, *1984*

Many fans today are aware that Babe Ruth was a pitcher before he became the home run king, but few realize just how remarkable a pitcher he was. As a left-hander he won 94 games and completed 107, and twice won more than 20 games in a season. He was the only major league player to achieve stardom as a pitcher and a hitter. Babe was on his way to the Hall of Fame as a pitcher until he was switched to the outfield, so that his batting strengths could be utilized daily.

George Herman Ruth got the nickname Babe in his first training camp in Fayetteville, North Carolina. Jack Dunn, the owner of the Baltimore Orioles (in 1914 they were a cut below the majors in the minor International League), signed him to a contract for $100 a month, and kept a close watch on George. He became known as Dunn's Baby and eventually Babe . . . which stuck. Soon he would also become known for his insatiable appetite, uncouth manners, and large ambition for baseball.

In 1914 Babe pitched for three months with a 14–6 record, but Jack Dunn was in financial trouble, so on July 9, 1914, he sold Babe to the Boston Red Sox with two other players for $22,500; Babe cost $2,900. Two days later Babe made his major league debut at Fenway Park against the Cleveland Indians, pitching seven innings and winning by a score of 4–3. In September of 1914, Ruth was sent to the minor league Providence Clam Diggers, a Red Sox farm team, to help them win the International League Pennant. In 1915, at the age of twenty, Babe rejoined the Red Sox as a regular starter and began his first full year as a major league player, on his way to making history a little bit at a time.

He was taught little because he didn't have to be taught much. The Babe pitched and won the first big league game he ever saw, a distinction few major leaguers can claim.

—TOM MEANY, Babe Ruth: The Big Moments and the Big Fella, *1947*

Just out of St. Mary's, Babe poses with his Oriole teammates on their way to spring training in Fayetteville, North Carolina. Babe is in the center of the back row, wearing the plaid cap (1914).

Babe had a natural flair for pitching baseballs. He showed all the earmarks of a great star almost from the very first time he donned an Oriole uniform. One of his most remarkable baseball achievements, and one which has been entirely overlooked, is that Ruth, still in his teens, was able to come out of an orphanage and, with no previous professional experience or coaching, become a winning pitcher in the International League.

—TOM MEANY, Babe Ruth: The Big Moments and the Big Fella, *1947*

When he was pitching he neither knew nor cared whether the batter who faced him stood at the right or left side of the plate, and when he was hitting he never took the time to distinguish between southpaws and right-handers. They all looked alike to Babe.

—TOM MEANY, Babe Ruth: The Big Moments and the Big Fella, *1947*

◆　　◆　　◆

"In 1919 Ed Barrow, then the Red Sox manager, made one of the wisest decisions in baseball history when he moved Babe Ruth permanently to the outfield. The great pitcher was now about to become the greatest slugger of all time."

—HARRY HOOPER, *Boston Red Sox teammate and right fielder, 1917,*
quoted in John Tullius, I'd Rather Be a Yankee, *1986*

◆　　◆　　◆

"I asked him if he would be willing to give up pitching and concentrate on the outfield. I told him he had a chance to become one of the greatest left-handers of all time, maybe the greatest, which was true. The Babe agreed to play the outfield principally, I think, because it got him into the game daily."

—ED BARROW, *Red Sox manager, quoted in John Tullius,* I'd Rather Be a Yankee, *1986*

By early July, his ability established, Dunn doubled his annual pay to $1,200 in May and raised it again to $1,800 in June. Ruth was flabbergasted: in February he was sleeping in a dorm with two hundred other kids, lucky to have a nickel in his pocket, and now barely six months later he was not only famous but rich too!

—LAWRENCE S. RITTER AND MARK RUCKER, The Babe: The Game That Ruth Built, *1997*

Babe (far right) leaning on catcher Ben Egan. The Baltimore International League Orioles, 1914.

"I went out and celebrated, just as soon as I got my first paycheck—$100. I bought a bicycle, something that I had wanted and often prayed for through most of my young life. Most of the Orioles, of course, had cars, but none of them was as proud as I was, riding the first possession of my life through the old streets of Baltimore."

—BABE RUTH, *as told to Bob Considine*, The Babe Ruth Story, *1948*

Baltimore. International.
1914

Babe in the front row (fifth from left). Owner and manager Jack Dunn is over Babe's right shoulder. Next to Babe on his right is Jack Dunn's son Jack Jr.

Certainly Ruth's natural ability was prodigious. He might have become the greatest of all—but baseball history would have been inconceivably different. On the other hand, imagine if they had the designated hitter rule in his day. Every fourth day he'd pitch (and bat). The other three he'd be the designated hitter. He'd wind up with 400 victories and 800 home runs, wouldn't he? And that would make him a double Hall of Famer.

—LEONARD KOPETT, The New Thinking Fan's Guide to Baseball

With his first major-league team, the Boston Red Sox, 1914

Ty Cobb argued with considerable logic that Babe's status as a pitcher in these early seasons was a significant help to his development as a home run hitter. "He could experiment at the plate. He didn't have to get a piece of the ball. He didn't have to protect the plate the way a regular batter was expected to. No one cares much if a pitcher strikes out or looks bad at bat, so Ruth could take that big swing. If he missed, it didn't matter. And when he didn't miss, the ball went a long way. As time went on, he learned more and more about how to control that big swing, and put the wood on the ball. By the time he became a full time outfielder, he was ready.

—ROBERT W. CREAMER, Babe: The Legend Comes to Life, *1974*

PITCHING HIGHLIGHTS

1914

Ruth became a star in his first start as an Oriole in April. He hit a single his first time at bat in organized ball. After he was sold to Boston, he appeared in five games, pitching in four. His record with Boston was 2–1 with a 3.91 ERA when he was sent to Providence of the International League. His International League record was 22–9.

1915–1919

Ruth was a regular starter for the Boston Red Sox as a left-hander. He was the starting and winning pitcher in his first three opening-day appearances as a Boston Red Sox in 1916, 1917, and 1918.

1915

Ruth's first full year in the majors as a regular starter. At the Polo Grounds on May 6, he hit his first major league home run against Jack Warhop of the Yankees. He had the best winning percentage in the league with a record of 18–8 and an ERA of 2.44.

1916

Ruth led the league with a 1.75 ERA and a 23–12 record. He also threw nine shutouts, which still stands as a major league record.

1917 Ruth had twenty-four wins and thirteen losses and an ERA of 2.01. He led the American League with thirty-five complete games and earned a $5,000 salary.

1918 The first year Ruth divided his time between pitching and the outfield. Still with the Boston Red Sox and making $7,000, he compiled a 13–7 record despite pitching half as often as he did in previous years. He had a 2.22 ERA, batted .300, and hit eleven home runs. In 1918 the regular season was over by Labor Day due to World War I. The Red Sox completed 126 of 154 originally scheduled games.

1919 Ruth had nine wins and five losses with a ERA of 2.97, but was a pitcher turned outfielder and began his rise to the top as a home run hitter, setting a new record with twenty-nine homers and earning a whopping $10,000. It was the first season he played more than a hundred games. Strapped for cash, the Red Sox owner, Harry Frazee, sold Ruth to the Yankees for the 1920 season.

As a pitcher in the regular season with the Red Sox, Ruth had eighty-nine wins and forty-six losses. Ruth pitched five games with the Yankees: 1920 (1), 1921 (2), 1930 (1), and 1933 (1). He won all five, the last two were complete games. He entered the record books with ninety-four wins and forty-six losses and an ERA of 2.28.

Babe was an outstanding
southpaw for the Red Sox. His
career Red Sox pitching record was
eighty-nine wins, forty-six losses.

WORLD SERIES PITCHING

Babe was at the top of his form in World Series games for the Boston Red Sox. In the three games that Ruth pitched from 1916–18 (one in 1916 and two in 1919), he threw 29⅔ innings without giving up a run, breaking Christy Mathewson's record of 28⅓ innings. He held the record for the consecutive scoreless innings in World Series play for forty-three years, until Yankee pitcher Whitey Ford broke it in 1961 with 33⅔ scoreless innings.

Here is the breakdown of Babe's 29⅔ scoreless innings:

◆ In the 1916 Boston Red Sox vs. Brooklyn Dodgers Series, Ruth pitched the second game, a fourteen-inning duel; he gave up one run in the first inning. No runs were scored off Babe from the second inning on, making a total of thirteen consecutive scoreless innings. The Red Sox won the game 2–1, and the Series 4–1. This remains the longest complete game pitching victory in World Series history. Babe gave up six hits in fourteen innings.

◆ The Red Sox returned to the World Series in 1918 to face the Chicago Cubs. The Series was started early, on September 5, due to World War I. Ruth pitched two games, the first and the fourth. In the first, he pitched nine scoreless innings, and the Red Sox won 1–0. He now had a total of twenty-two scoreless innings. It was not until the final out of the eighth inning of his next game that he gave up a run, making the final total 29⅔ consecutive scoreless innings.

◆ With Ruth, the Red Sox won three World Series titles in five years.

    1915   4–1   Against Philadelphia (he did not pitch)

    1916   4–1   Against Brooklyn

    1918   4–2   Against Chicago

The Red Sox have not won the World Series since, thus the genesis of the "Curse of the Bambino."

◆ In 1915 the Red Sox beat the Philadelphia Phillies 4–1 in the World Series. Babe did not pitch and was at bat once without a hit. His winner's share was $3,780.25, which was more than his salary. He used some of the money to set his father up with a saloon.

◆ On September 5, 1918, during the seventh-inning stretch, the band played the "Star-Spangled Banner" for the first time. Ruth was on the mound warming up. The song, which was not the national anthem at the time, was so well received that it was played during the seventh inning stretch in the next two games in Chicago, and then before the start of the games in Boston. The "Star-Spangled Banner" became the national anthem by an Act of Congress in 1931 and since then it has been played at every major league game.

◆ In the 1918 Series against the Chicago Cubs, Ruth was the only starting pitcher in history to bat anywhere but ninth in the order. In Game 4 Ruth batted sixth. He grounded out, hit a two-run triple, and sacrificed. Catcher Sam Agnew was Boston's ninth-place batter.

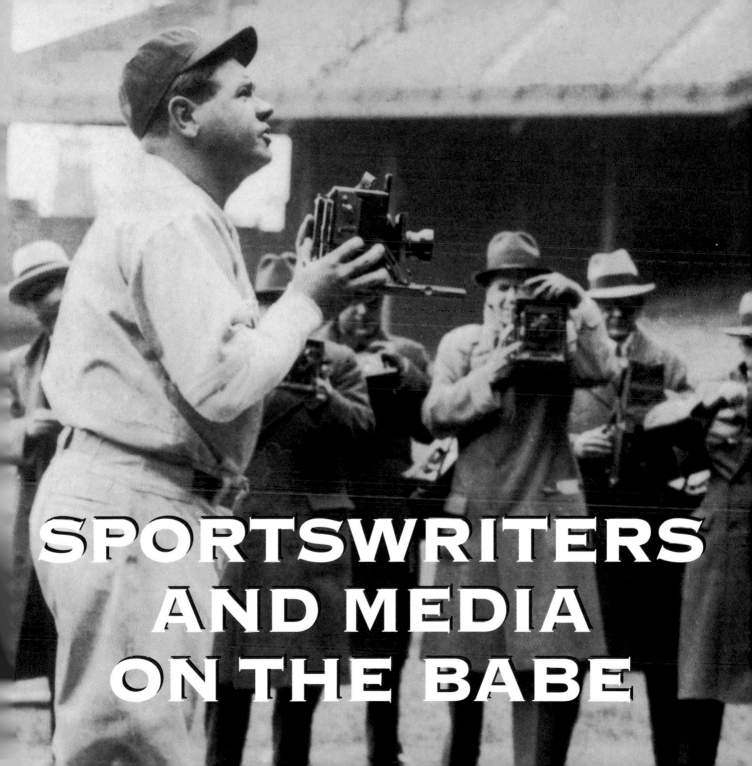

SPORTSWRITERS
AND MEDIA
ON THE BABE

Babe Ruth! That's all anyone had to hear. He was the biggest thing in the world. He was the loudest noise in a land made mute by poverty and unemployment. Long before Palmer or Jordan, Woods or Ali, Babe Ruth smothered America with his presence. And he did it at a time where there was no television, computers, cell phones, Internet, coffee bars or ESPN. He was a walking talking highlight film each and every day of his life, both on and off the field, most of it created and nurtured through word of mouth, a mountain of newspaper stories and the fact that he was the most marvelous ballplayer of all time.

—Mike Barnicle, ESPN the Magazine, *September 14, 1999*

Babe's personality was perfectly suited for the spotlight and his actions both on and off the field were the subject of constant media attention. Everything he did was scrutinized and the sportswriters and play-by-play announcers loved to dramatize his magic and mystique. Babe was always primed to supply new material for stories. That was the beauty of Babe.

Babe being interviewed by one of the great announcers, Graham McNamee

In the 1920s, there were over twenty daily newspapers in New York, each costing about 5 cents. Before radio, newspapers were the main source of information and it was common for people to wait in line at newsstands throughout the night to be one of the first to read about Babe and the Yankees. Baseball was America's favorite pastime—football, basketball, and hockey were not as popular as they are now.

The first radio play-by-play of a Yankee game was the opening game of the New York Yankees vs. New York Giants World Series in 1922 at the Polo Grounds. WJZ, a Newark, New Jersey, station, linked wires to the Polo Grounds, and the game and the rest of the Series were heard over the airwaves in the Eastern section of the country. The cheers and shouts that greeted Babe as he came to bat made the radio listeners feel as if they were a part of the game. The recordings and recollections of sportswriters and broadcasters then and now continue to keep Babe's legacy very much alive.

"**Every reporter that covered Ruth had the illusion that he was a great friend of Ruth, a personal friend. The minute he started to write about Ruth he was writing about what he considered to be his friend.**"

—JEAN SHEPHERD, *quoted in* Babe Ruth, *HBO Documentary, 1998*

To watch Ruth go down, swinging from the heels, often sprawling from the sheer violence of his cut, was almost as exciting as seeing him blast one out of the park.

—GRANTLAND RICE, *sportswriter and author,* The Tumult and the Shouting, *1954*

◆   ◆   ◆

"He had the most famous face in the world. If he appeared out of the grave today, everyone would know who he was."

—RAY ROBINSON, *sportswriter,* New York Times, *quoted in Bill Koenig,*
USA Today Baseball Weekly, *August 12, 1998*

How did Ruth become almost mythological? You can start with the round face. Round and joyous, an invitation to the dance.

—Bill Koenig, USA Today Baseball Weekly, *August 1998*

Suppose Ruth had more frequently gone to bed early, and with Mrs. Ruth. Suppose he had not downed a couple of hot dogs (and a glass of bicarbonate soda) before most games. Suppose he had not had the habits that caused him to balloon one winter to a gargantuan 49¾-inch waist—larger than his chest. (Perhaps the Yankees would not be wearing pinstripes today, an innovation ordered by their owner, the elegant Jacob Ruppert, who hoped the stripes would make Ruth look less obese.) If Ruth had lived sensibly and trained as we now know how to train, he would loom even larger over his era, like an Everest in Kansas.

—George F. Will, Men at Work: The Craft of Baseball, *1990*

Yankee owner Jacob Ruppert with Babe; both are in pinstripes. Although some say it's a myth, others say it's a fact that Ruppert added pinstripes to the Yankee uniform permanently in 1927 to make Babe look thinner.

"His existence enlarges us just by looking at him, thinking about him, because you saw perfection. It was so glorious, it was almost painful. You were at the ballpark and Babe took that swing and the ball didn't fall down in the end, it whacked against a seat in the bleachers. I saw this, I was here, I was in the presence of greatness. And to be in the presence of greatness means that some tiny fleck of it is attached to you."

—HAYWOOD HALE BROUN, *quoted in* Babe Ruth,
HBO Documentary, 1998

"As baseball's biggest draw Ruth made a fortune across the country. No town was too small or too far away. If the Babe's fans could not come to a game he would get to them. He was spreading baseball across the country."

—Babe Ruth, *HBO Documentary, 1998*

❖　　❖　　❖

He played his last game nearly 65 years ago, yet he still is the most famous player in the only big-league sport that spanned the century. He dominated the golden era of sports, he was the original larger-than-life sports hero and he became the first of many athletes to be known on a first-name basis.

You say "20th Century," I say "The Babe."

—CHRISTINE BRENNAN, *"First Dominant Hero Still No. 1: The Babe,"*
USA Today, *December 31, 1999*

41

Even boarding the train to spring training was a major media event. Babe is on the left sitting on the rail. Lou Gehrig is at the other end of the rail.

"**B**abe and I and two other guys were playing bridge. Babe was sitting next to the window. A woman with a little baby in her arms came up and started peering at the Babe. She was rather good looking. Babe looked at her and went on playing bridge. Then he looked at her again and finally he leaned out and said, 'Better get away from here lady, I'll put one in the other arm.'"

—RICHARDS VIDNER, *sportswriter*, New York Times, *on a train making a stop in an Illinois station, quoted in Jerome Holtzman*, The Armchair Book of Baseball

There is no question that Ruth had an instinctive flair for the game. He proved this hundreds of times by bunting when the opposition expected him to pull for the fence, by hitting to the opposite field to prevent over-shifting against him and, in his younger days, daringly trying for an extra base.

—TOM MEANY, Babe Ruth: The Big Moments and the Big Fella, *1947*

43

Ruth was a good base runner until his tonnage caught up with him. He often stole better than ten a season, twice getting as many as seventeen, and stealing bases calls for more than speed alone. A successful base stealer must be a good observer; he must know when to break on a pitcher. All this the big fellow could do.

—Tom Meany, Babe Ruth: The Big Moments and the Big Fella, *1947*

◆　　◆　　◆

Signs, however, remained a black art to the Babe. That mysterious phase of baseball whereby a coach touches his hand to his ear, to the insignia on his uniform, to the peak of his cap, etc., to inform the batter that he is to take or hit at the next pitch never made any impression on Ruth. Whatever he may have done with the Red Sox as a young fellow, Babe never took or gave a sign in all of his fifteen seasons with the Yankees. It wasn't the handicap it might seem. There was no sense in picking out a ball for him to hit, because Babe had better eyes for that than any one who ever played. And there was no need for Ruth to signal ahead to the base runner that he was going to put on the hit-and-run, because when Babe hit the runner rarely needed a head start.

—Tom Meany, Babe Ruth: The Big Moments and the Big Fella, *1947*

A slightly overweight Babe could still get
down low for the slide.

It wasn't just that Ruth had dominated the sport for most of his twenty-two years in it. Nor that he had played in 2,503 major league games, gone to bat 8,399 times, made 2,873 hits, scored 2,174 runs and closed his career with a batting average of .342. Nor that he had excelled as a pitcher before becoming a great hitter. Nor that he had rescued the game from the disaster of the Black Sox scandal of the 1919 World Series. Nor that he had "built" Yankee Stadium and the modern Yankees.

Ruth's real role was even broader: By hitting 714 home runs and revolutionizing the image of baseball, he had elevated the game itself, raised the sights and salaries of all players along with his own, raised the revenues of all clubs—and captured the public's imagination with the style and stuff of legends.

—JOSEPH DURSO, DiMaggio: The Last American Knight, *1995*

You think McGwire and Sosa gave baseball a shot in the arm? Babe gave the game a 714 home run Heimlich maneuver. The Black Sox threw the 1919 World Series and Carl Mays killed a player with a pitch in 1920, but because of Babe, baseball thrived.

—JIM CAPLE, Sport *magazine*, *December 1999*

It was impossible to watch him at bat without experiencing an emotion. I have seen hundreds of ballplayers at the plate, and none of them managed to convey the message of impending doom to a pitcher that Babe Ruth did with the cock of his head, the position of his legs and the little gentle waving of the bat, feathered in his two big paws.

—PAUL GALLICO, New York Daily News, *1927*

◆　◆　◆

He had a violent swing. And if he missed, he'd cork screw in the batter's box and wind up facing the grandstand. He looked like a beer keg on stilts. And when he hit a homer, he'd round the bases with a unique mincing gait, doffing his cap, grinning with child-like exuberance.

—STAN HOCHMAN, Philadelphia Daily News, *August 1998*

Ruth was the first national superstar—the man who gave us that category.

—GEORGE F. WILL, *author and columnist, in* Outside the Lines:
Babe Ruth's Larger Than Life Legacy, *ESPN Documentary, 1998*

◆　　◆　　◆

Miller Huggins who won six pennants, had a tough crew to handle, headed by a young Babe Ruth when he was just emerging as a star. In Ruth, Miller had two tigers by their tails, for Babe would accept a $5,000 fine and a long suspension with a grin.

GRANTLAND RICE, *sportswriter and author,* The Tumult and the Shouting, *1954*

"He had an idea how to merchandise himself. He understood the importance of the media, long before most players did. He understood radio's impact. It was new, startling. It put the premium on personality—and whose personality could be better suited than Ruth's?"

—CURT SMITH, *quoted in Bill Koenig,* USA Today Baseball Weekly, *August 12–18, 1998*

The Bambino over the radio air waves

I've seen the great ones, from Cobb through Williams, but Ruth was the only ball player I have known who could turn out capacity crowds every time. He did this in every city the Yankees played.

—GRANTLAND RICE, *sportswriter and author,* The Tumult and the Shouting, *1954*

◆　　◆　　◆

The Babe was his own marketing machine. He didn't need agents or publicists to make himself a household name. He did it all by himself, always with a keen and underestimated eye too.

—MIKE BARNICLE, ESPN the Magazine, *September 14, 1999*

51

Outside of Charles Chaplin, I do not know of
an entertainer who has provided more
enjoyment than the Babe, and if there were
any way of appraising the drawing power of the
Babe I think that he would be shown to be the
greatest money maker as an entertainer for all
time.

—W. O. MCGEEHAN, New York Herald-Tribune,
June 6, 1927

◆   ◆   ◆

Babe Ruth was the first marketing superstar.

He created the media circus.

—MICKEY PAXTON, *senior media director, J. Walter Thompson*
Advertising Agency

I'm sure no ballplayer had so much to do with the swift, sure success of a team as did Ruth with the Yankees. And yet, at the same time, I feel the Babe was indebted to New York for providing him with an appropriate stage for his tremendous heroics. The greatest figure the game has known needed baseball's greatest team, and vice versa. The Yankees probably would have become the fabulous success they are now without the Babe, but, I'm certain, the road to the top would have been much longer and much less exciting.

—GRANTLAND RICE, Sport *magazine, September 1951*

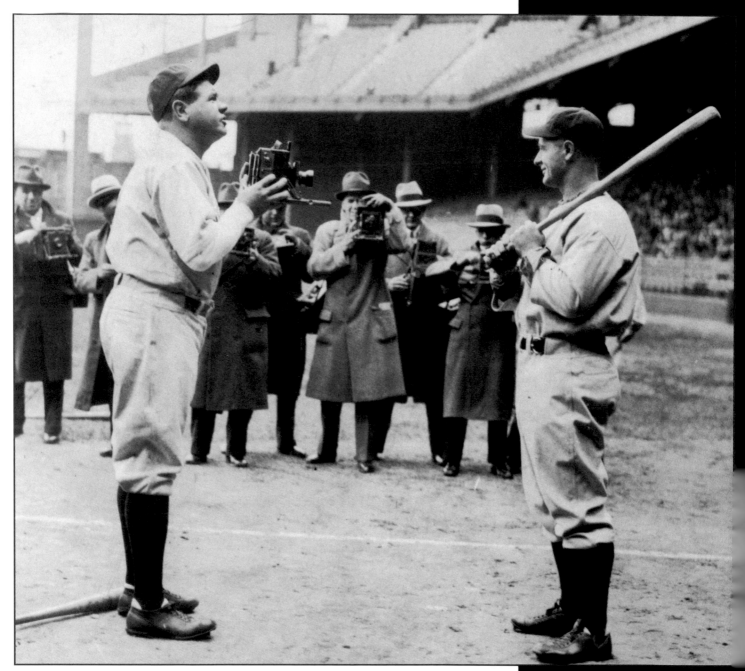
Hamming it up for the media with Lou Gehrig

"**If** Babe Ruth were alive today, he'd be Mark McGwire, Ken Griffey Jr. and Sammy Sosa—rolled into one."

—BILL KOENIG, *quoted in* USA Today Baseball Weekly, *August 12–18, 1998*

Both teammates and opponents of Ruth vividly remember the times when they played with or against him. To be able to say that they played in a game with Babe Ruth gives them a special pride and satisfaction. In their old age, it is apparent that they believe just having been on the same field with him validates their own careers, indeed to some extent their own lives. And that, after all is said and done, is the ultimate testimony to his greatness.

—LAWRENCE S. RITTER AND MARK RUCKER, The Babe: The Game That Ruth Built, *1997*

Number 1 on the Top 100 Players of the Century is Babe Ruth: His records might fall, but no one player comes close to his place in history.

Pick your stat, identify your criteria and make your case. Then step back and pay homage to The Bambino—Ruth—the greatest player of the 20th century. Twist and tweak the numbers any way you like. Hits, homers and RBI. Batting, on-base and slugging.

Then remember Ruth was more than The Sultan of Swat. He very well could have been The Monarch of the Mound, as his 94–46 pitching record and 2.28 earned run average show.

That's why Ruth easily sits atop the Century Survey, a compilation by the Society for American Baseball Research of the 100 greatest major league players.

—PAUL WHITE, USA Today Baseball Weekly, *June 23–29, 1999*

PLAYERS
AND MANAGERS
ON THE BABE

"Now Babe Ruth, he was different. What a warm-hearted, generous soul he was. Always friendly, always time for a laugh or a wise-crack. The Babe always had a twinkle in his eye, and when he'd hit a homer against us he'd never trot past third without giving me a wink.

"The Babe would give you the shirt off his back. All you had to do was ask him. The big fellow wasn't perfect. Everybody knows that. But that guy had a heart. He really did. A heart as big as a watermelon, and made out of pure gold."

—JIMMY AUSTIN, *St. Louis Brown third baseman, quoted in Lawrence S. Ritter,* The Glory of Their Times, *1984*

Just about everyone connected to baseball—players, managers, and coaches—was awed by Babe's amazing strength and infectious enthusiasm for baseball. Considering he was such an overwhelming star, it would have been easy for other players to be envious—but in reality most got "a big kick" out of Babe. They enjoyed his candor and showmanship. After all, Babe's popularity boosted attendance around the league, which helped pay their salaries. Babe was very much aware of his fame but did not let it interfere with his friendships. He enjoyed socializing with his baseball buddies over the years and provided them with many memorable moments.

◆   ◆   ◆

"Ball players weren't the celebrities that they came to be later on, with a few exceptions, of course like Cobb and Walter Johnson. But the Babe changed that. He changed everything, that guy. So many, many people became interested in baseball because of him. They would be drawing 1,500 a game in St. Louis. We'd go in there with the Babe and they'd be all over the ballpark; there would be mounted police riding the crowd back. Thousands and thousands of people coming out to see that one guy. Whatever the owners paid him, it wasn't enough—it couldn't be enough."

—ROGER PECKINPAUGH, *New York Yankee shortstop 1913–21,*
quoted in John Tullius, I'd Rather Be a Yankee, *1986*

Barnstorming team "Bustin Babes" playing a Japanese
American team in Fresno, California, in 1927

"**D**on't tell me about Ruth;
I've seen what he did to
people. I've seen them, fans
driving miles in open wag-
ons through the prairies of
Oklahoma to see him in
exhibition games as we
headed north in the spring.
I've seen them: kids, men,
women, worshippers all,
hoping to get his name on a
torn, dirty piece of paper, or
hoping for a grunt of
recognition when they said,
'Hi ya, Babe.' He never let
them down; not once. He
was the greatest crowd
pleaser of them all."

—WAITE HOYT, *New York Yankee pitcher,*
1921–30, and Ruth's friend,
quoted in John Tullius, I'd Rather
Be a Yankee, *1986*

"Babe Ruth joined us in the middle of 1914, a nineteen-year-old kid. He was a left-handed pitcher then, and a good one. He had never been anywhere, didn't know anything about manners or how to behave among people, just a big overgrown green pea. You probably remember him with that big belly he got later on. But that wasn't there in 1914. George was six foot two, and weighed 198 pounds, all of it muscle. He had a slim waist, huge biceps, no self-discipline, and not much education—not so very different from a lot of other nineteen-year-old would-be ball players. Except for two things: he could eat more than anyone else, and he could hit a baseball further."

—HARRY HOOPER, *Boston Red Sox teammate and right fielder, 1917,*
quoted in Lawrence S. Ritter, The Glory of Their Times

"When Ruth's time at bat is over and it's my turn the fans are still buzzing about what Babe did, regardless of whether he belted a home run or struck out. They wouldn't notice it if I walked up to home plate on my hands, stood on my head, and held the bat between my toes."

—LOU GEHRIG, *New York Yankee first baseman, 1923–39, quoted in Lawrence S. Ritter and Mark Rucker,* The Babe: The Game That Ruth Built, *1997*

◆ ◆ ◆

"Not many guys looked good striking out, but the Babe did."

—PHIL RIZZUTO, *New York Yankee shortstop, 1941–42, 1946–56, then television announcer*

◆ ◆ ◆

Walter Johnson was victimized for three home runs in Ruth's record fifty-nine home runs in 1921. When asked years later to compare the length of Ruth's blasts to that of Jimmie Foxx and Hank Greenberg. Johnson replied "All I can say is that the balls Ruth hit out of the park got smaller quicker than anybody else's."

—WALTER JOHNSON, *Washington Senator pitcher, 1907–1927, quoted by sportswriter Shirley Povich,* Washington Post, *March 13, 1989*

"In Philadelphia in those days, back of the right field wall there was a street, then a line of those houses that are all the same with those marble steps, then back of that another line of houses.

"Well now, Babe had the fastest set of reflexes I've ever known on a batter. So I put one over in his hands and the Babe hit the ball and he did hit it! I'm standing there on the mound watching the ball, forgetting all about the ball game and the fact that the home run was being hit off me. I was just amazed at the tremendous distance that ball was carrying and I thought, 'By George, that's the longest home run I ever seen.'

"And here I am, in complete amazement, sheer astonishment, standing on the mound and there goes the ball out over the right field wall, over the first row of houses and hit in the second street beyond.

"Then all of a sudden, I remembered that the ball was hit off me and, by George, was I mad."

—WAITE HOYT, *Philadelphia Athletic pitcher, 1931, New York Yankee pitcher, 1921–30, quoted in John Tullius,* I'd Rather Be a Yankee, *1986*

"Babe Ruth could hit a ball so hard, and so far it was sometimes impossible to believe your eyes. To give you an example, in 1920, he hit 50 home runs and everybody else in the whole rest of the league added together hit only about 300. About one in every seven home runs hit in the American League that year was hit by Babe Ruth.

"My God if he was playing today. If Babe was as good relative to everybody else today like he used to be, he'd hit over 200 home runs a season. Take Mantle, Mays, Killebrew and take anyone else you want to name today and add them all up and they still won't match Ruth's home runs relative to the rest of the league."

—SAM JONES, *pitcher, Ruth's teammate on the Boston Red Sox, 1916–21, and the New York Yankees, 1922–26, quoted in Lawrence S. Ritter,* The Glory of Their Times, *1984*

Babe was unique. He ate and drank as he pleased. He was the fans' favorite, and he always came through in the clutch. Everybody admired him. When we went to Yankee Stadium, Babe would come out last, and everybody on the field would stop what they were doing and watch him take batting practice. I never saw anything like it in my whole life.

—HANK GREENBERG, *Detroit Tiger first baseman, 1930, 1933–41,* The Story of My Life, *1989*

"He was the one, the first one, the biggest one to bring recognition to the sport and make it what it has become today. So everyone knows Babe Ruth, they know what he looks like and they know how many home runs he hit."

—CAL RIPKIN JR., *Baltimore Oriole shortstop, 1981–present*

◆　　◆　　◆

I never put myself in Ruth's class as a home-run hitter. He was head and shoulders above any home-run hitter in baseball in my era, and certainly he's in a class by himself for all time. His 714 home runs in a twenty-two year career—the first four years as a pitcher—were hit in 3,993 fewer times at bat than Hank Aaron, who broke the record and finished with 755 home runs after playing twenty-three years. That's not to take away from Aaron's home run record, but certainly if the Babe had played in the current baseball climate with the leagues expanded to twenty-six teams and the talent watered down, there's no telling how many home runs he would have hit.

—HANK GREENBERG, *Detroit Tiger first baseman, 1930, 1933–41,*
The Story of My Life, *1989*

"I like to pitch to Babe better than to anybody else in base-ball. And I consider him the most dangerous of all batters. Why do I like to pitch to Babe? Because he is a never-ending puzzle. You always have to extend yourself to the utmost when you face Babe. Sometimes he looks very easy, but there is one thing it is never safe for a pitcher to bank on. Any time he figures that he has Babe's number he is feeding himself a liberal dose of misplaced confidence."

—URBAN SHOCKER, *pitcher in 1923, coming off his fourth consecutive twenty-win season for the St. Louis Browns, quoted in* Baseball Weekly, *November 1923*

◆　◆　◆

"All the lies about Ruth are true."

—WAITE HOYT, *New York Yankee pitcher 1921–30, as told to Robert W. Creamer, quoted in Bill Koenig,* USA Today Baseball Weekly, *August 1998*

"Ruth was the most destructive force in Baseball. I don't mean the force of Ruth's homers alone. The mere presence of Babe created a disastrous psychological problem for the other team."

—MILLER HUGGINS, *New York Yankee manager, 1918–29, quoted in John Tullius,* I'd Rather Be a Yankee, *1986*

Lou Gehrig, Russell "Buzz" Arlett of the International League Orioles, and Babe at old Oriole Park circa 1932

Members of the music industry, from New York to California, were also big fans of Babe.

"There is one thing that Babe can always be counted on to supply. He gives the opposing pitcher a thrill no matter what happens. If you strike him out you get a very pleasurable thrill, as long as it lasts. If he hits you for a solid smash you get another kind of thrill; why do cowboys ride wild steers and risk their necks on bucking broncos? It is a dangerous sport but it gives them a thrill, I suppose, to think they have conquered something which was strong and reckless and hard to handle."

—*Urban Shocker*, St. Louis Brown pitcher, Baseball Weekly, *November 1923*

◆   ◆   ◆

"Honestly, at one time I thought Babe Ruth was a cartoon character. I really did, I mean, I wasn't born until 1961, and I grew up in Indiana."

—Don Mattingly, *New York Yankee first baseman, 1982–95, quoted in the* Sporting News

"Wives of ball players, when they teach their children their prayers, should instruct them to say God Bless Mommy, God Bless Daddy, God Bless Babe Ruth. Babe has upped Daddy's paychecks by fifteen to forty percent."

—WAITE HOYT, *New York Yankee pitcher, 1921–1930, and Ruth's friend, quoted in Robert Lipsyte and Peter Levine,* Idols of the Game, *1995*

"Ain't no man who ever lived that can play the part of Babe Ruth off the playing field. He was the only guy that ever lived up to his reputation."

—TOMMY HENRICH, *New York Yankee player and coach, in* Babe Ruth, *HBO Documentary, 1998*

◆　◆　◆

"When I first played the game they couldn't play on the Sabbath because that was the preachers' day to collect. I still remember my first game against Babe Ruth and that day he hit two over my head and then I knew who Babe Ruth was."

—CASEY STENGEL, *New York Giant outfielder, 1921–23, New York Yankee manager, 1949–60, New York Mets manager, 1962–65, from his acceptance speech when he was inducted into the Baseball Hall of Fame, July 25, 1966*

Babe was adored by kids everywhere.
Japan, 1934.

"Ruth isn't a man; he is an institution."

—MOE BERG, *catcher, Chicago White Sox, 1926–30, Washington Senators, 1932–34, Boston Red Sox, 1935–39, quoted in Grantland Rice,* The Tumult and The Shouting, *1954*

There's no question that the competition was keener in those days. Despite the influx later of great black players, the talent overall then was more concentrated. The reason is, almost all the athletes turned to baseball. There were no other professional athletics to speak of. Football was in its infancy, basketball was nonexistent, tennis was for the newly rich or ne'er-do-wells, and hockey was a Canadian sport that hadn't invaded the United States. Baseball was the game, and all the athletes who had any talent at all tried to make a career in professional baseball. That was the kind of competition the Babe was up against.

—HANK GREENBERG, *Detroit Tiger first baseman, 1930, 1933–41,*
The Story of My Life, *1989*

◆　◆　◆

"He was quite a guy, always a lot of fun. All the guys really liked him, and, Lord, could he hit a baseball. I remember one of those late-season exhibition games one October back around 1929 at the old Baker Bowl in Philadelphia. The right-field fence wasn't far away, but Broad Street was a real wide street, and there was a train station on the opposite side. Well, twice in that game Ruth hit balls so far to right field that they almost cleared the train station. I've seen a lot of long drives in my time— gunlike—Josh Gibson, "Mule" Suttles, Turkey Sterns, and Jimmie Foxx, but I believe those two balls Babe hit that day were the longest I've ever seen. He was some kind of guy."

—WILLIAM "JUDY" JOHNSON, *Hall of Fame, Negro League Hilldale, Homestead Gray, and Pittsburgh Crawford third baseman, 1921–38, as told to baseball historian Bill Jenkinson on June 5, 1987*

"One of the thrills in my career was when I was delegated to go with the American [All-Star] baseball team to Japan . . . The Japanese were literally crazy about baseball and walked miles to see the American athletes. Every game was sold out at least three weeks in advance. Ruth was their idol.

"The Japanese even began to get up before daylight to play at sunrise. One day when we went out about twenty miles from the city to practice in a place where there were no houses, about twenty thousand came to watch us."

—CONNIE MACK, *Philadelphia Athletic manager and owner, 1901–50,*
quoted in John Tullius, I'd Rather Be a Yankee, *1986*

◆　◆　◆

The team was paraded down the Ginza in Tokyo in open cars, with the Babe's in front. Fans crowded so tightly around his car that the whole cavalcade came to a dead stop. Newspapers reported that more than a million people had come out to see Ruth. Charlie Gehringer, in an interview years later, remembered the reception well. "It seemed like all Tokyo was out, waving and yelling. We could hardly get our cars through, the streets were so jammed. What was interesting was that they knew who we all were. You'd think being so many miles away and being [of] such a different culture, the whole thing would have been strange to them. But apparently they'd been following big league baseball for years and gee, they knew us all. Especially Ruth, of course. They made a terrific fuss over him, and he loved it."

—*"Lefty O'Doul and the Development of Japanese Baseball,"*
in Richard Leutzinger, The National Pastime

No gimmick was too
extreme for Babe.
Japan, 1934.

"Now, I've had everything except the thrill of watching Babe Ruth play."

—JOE DIMAGGIO, *New York Yankee center fielder, 1936–42, on being inducted into the Baseball Hall of Fame in 1955*

Babe, Bill Corum, and a young Joe DiMaggio at a sportswriters dinner in New York, January 1937

"I don't want them to forget Ruth. I just want them to remember me!"

—HANK AARON, *frequently heard quote as he got close to breaking Babe's lifetime home run record*

"Indeed, the name Babe Ruth has become synonymous with baseball. One can hardly talk about the game without talking about the Babe. His legacy endures. For decades his record of 714 home runs was thought unbeatable. And quite frankly, it was not until I had hit 600 home runs that the thought crossed my mind that I might be able to challenge the record."

—HANK AARON, *who broke Babe's all-time home run record, quoted in Lawrence S. Ritter and Mark Rucker,* The Babe: The Game That Ruth Built, *1997*

◆　◆　◆

I never saw the ball hit so hard before or since. He was fat and old, but he still had that great swing. Even when he missed, you could hear that bat go swish. I can't remember anything about the first home run he hit off me that day. I guess it was just another homer. But I can't forget that last one. It's probably still going."

—GUY BUSH, *Pittsburgh Pirate pitcher on May 25, 1935—home runs 713 and 714 hit off him, quoted in Bill Koenig,* USA Today Baseball Weekly, *August 1998*

David Wells of the New York Yankees pitched a perfect game on May 17, 1998, against the Minnesota Twins. A few weeks later on June 28, he met Don Larsen for the first time before the Yankee-Met game at Shea Stadium. Larsen, age sixty-eight, had pitched a perfect game for the Yankees on October 8, 1956, in the World Series against the Brooklyn Dodgers. Ironically both attended Point Loma High School in San Diego, California.

"I saw Babe Ruth hit once," Larsen said, and Wells' eyes lit up like a child's.

"I was 7 or 8 or 9," Larsen said. "It was an exhibition in Indiana."

"Did he crank one?" Wells asked.

"He cranked a couple." Larsen said.

—BRIAN LEWIS, New York Post, *June 29, 1998*

David Wells, now pitching for Toronto, is a Ruth fanatic. When he joined the Yankees in 1997 he requested Number 3 for his uniform. Since the Babe's number had been retired for almost fifty years Wells chose Number 33. Wells is a collector of baseball memorabilia, and owns one of Babe Ruth's original caps and wore it in a game in June of 1998. He paid a reputed $35,000 for it. Wells also owns a ball signed by Ruth.

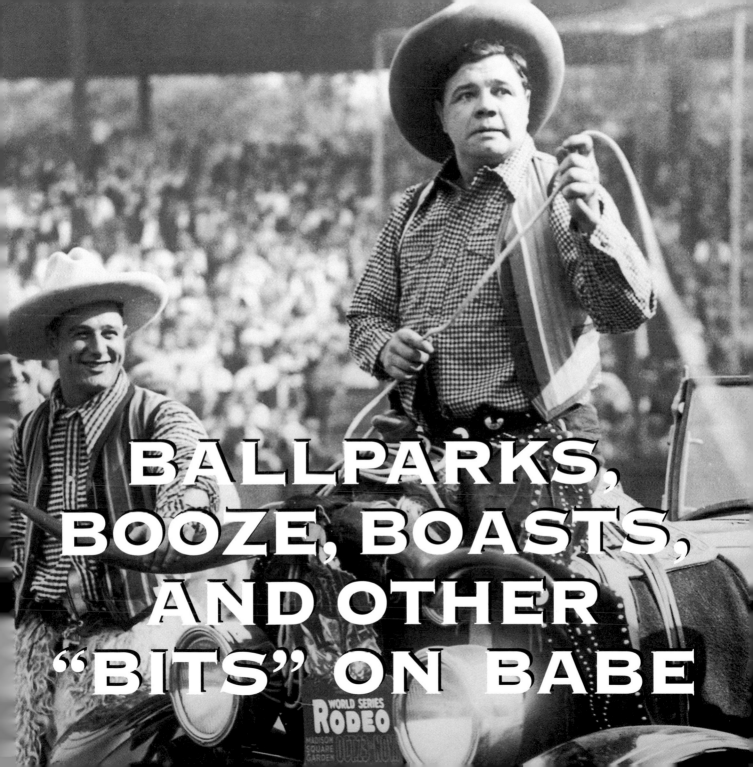

BALLPARKS, BOOZE, BOASTS, AND OTHER "BITS" ON BABE

WORLD SERIES
RODEO
MADISON
SQUARE
GARDEN

Babe transcended sport in the sense that people who didn't care about sports knew who he was. He went outside of the limits of sport culture.

He was loved because people who had flaws, men, women and even children who had flaws in their character, knew he had flaws. He was one of them, not above them.

—Babe Ruth, *HBO Documentary, 1998*

The numbers tell only part of the story . . . the enigma that was Babe Ruth had many sides. Filled with an abundance of energy and relentless ambition, there was nothing conventional about Babe. He more or less invented himself as he went along, and he always enjoyed who he was. Babe first became known for his thunderous home runs, but soon all aspects of his life held the public's fascination. The cumulative parts made for a very colorful character.

Construction [on Yankee Stadium] began in February 1922, and after a year of feverish work, the grand structure was completed in time for Opening Day, April 23, 1923.

Over 74,000 fans jammed the stadium that day, and police had to turn back another 25,000, easily the largest crowd that had ever seen a game. Always primed for the drama of an important moment, the Babe christened "the House that Ruth built" by hitting a three-run homer to win the game for the Yankees, 4–1.

—JOHN TULLIUS, I'd Rather Be a Yankee, *1986*

◆   ◆   ◆

No man on earth had more nicknames than George Herman Ruth. The Babe. The Man. The Bambino. The Home Run King. The Circuit Smasher. Herman the Great. Homeric Herman. The Bulky Monarch. The King of Clout. His Eminence. The Sultan of Swat.

—*"Babe Ruth,"* Sports Illustrated, *September 1998*

◆   ◆   ◆

Beyond Ruth's astounding athletic achievements, he became an American phenomenon. He brought people to the game who had never seen or cared about baseball before. They wanted to see Babe Ruth, to watch him hit one of his tremendous blasts, and when he did, a new fan was born.

—JOHN TULLIUS, I'd Rather Be a Yankee, *1986*

He [Babe] was sitting around a table with several players and their wives in Hot Springs in 1923.

"Excuse me," he said getting up, "I've got to take a piss."

Herb Pennock, very much a gentleman and also very much a friend of Ruth's, followed Babe out to the men's room. "Babe, you shouldn't say that in front of the ladies."

"Say what?"

"Say piss like that. You just don't say that in front of women. You should say, excuse me, I have to go to the bathroom, or something like that."

They went back to the table and sat down, and Ruth said to the women, "I'm sorry I said piss."

—ROBERT W. CREAMER, Babe: The Legend Comes to Life, *1974*

"The Chicago White Sox got a great idea, they were going to take the Babe out. They're going to make a night of it.

"Three minutes before the ball game, and here comes the Babe. Miller Huggins [Yankee manager] doesn't even look at him, but says, 'He hasn't even been in bed all night. He's going to play today.'

"Oh, and he played, he butchered the White Sox.

"When the game was over, Babe hurried up the steps to get to the White Sox before they disappeared. 'Hey, where are we going tonight?'"

—TOMMY HENRICH, *New York Yankee right fielder, 1937–42, and coach, 1946–50, in* Babe Ruth, HBO Documentary, *1998*

The bartender put a couple of fistfuls of ice chunks into a big, thick mixing glass and then proceeded to make a Tom Collins that had so much gin in it that the other people at the bar started to laugh. He served the drink to the Babe just as it was made, right in the mixing glass.

Ruth said something about how heavens to Betsy hot he was, and then he picked up the glass and opened his mouth, and there went everything. In one shot he swallowed the drink, the orange slice and the rest of the garbage, and the ice chunks too. He stopped for nothing. There is not a single man I have ever seen in a saloon who does not bring his teeth together a little bit and stop those ice chunks from going in. A man has to have a pipe the size of a trombone to take ice in one shot. But I saw Ruth do it, and whenever somebody tells me about how the Babe used to drink and eat when he was playing ball, I believe every word of it.

—JIMMY BRESLIN, Can't Anybody Here Play This Game?

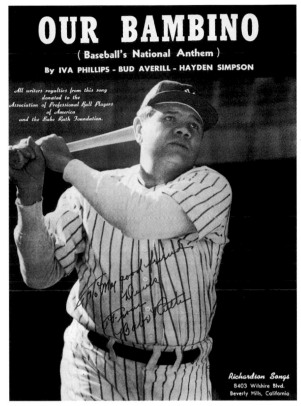

More than fifteen songs were published in tribute to the Bambino.

Signing his contract with Yankee owner Jacob
Ruppert. Although a lefty, Babe wrote with
his right hand.

And so Ruth had a two-year contract at $80,000. The impact of $80,000 in 1930 is lost against the background of the vast amounts paid today's professional stars. But here are verified figures for salaries earned a couple of seasons earlier by the 1927 Yankees, that team of superstars. After Ruth, at $70,000, the next highest paid player was Pennock, at $17,500. Meusel made $13,000, Dugan and Hoyt $12,000, Combs $10,000. Gehrig made $8,000, Lazzeri $8,000, Koenig $7,000. Wilcy Moore, who won 19 games, got $3,000.

The President of the United States, as stories about Ruth so often point out, was paid $75,000 in 1931. The idea of a ballplayer making more than the President was almost incomprehensible. An apocryphal story, often told, says that someone asked Ruth if he thought it was right for him to be paid more than President Hoover and that Ruth replied, "Why not? I had a better year than he did."

—ROBERT W. CREAMER, Babe: The Legend Comes to Life, *1974*

Babe always had fun
entertaining crowds.

Ruth was a man who loved crowds. And the crowds always swarmed to see Babe hit. The Yankees from 1926 to 1934 were a terrific aggregation, each man big in his own right. But it was Babe the crowds came to see.

—Grantland Rice, *sportswriter and author,*
The Tumult and the Shouting, *1954*

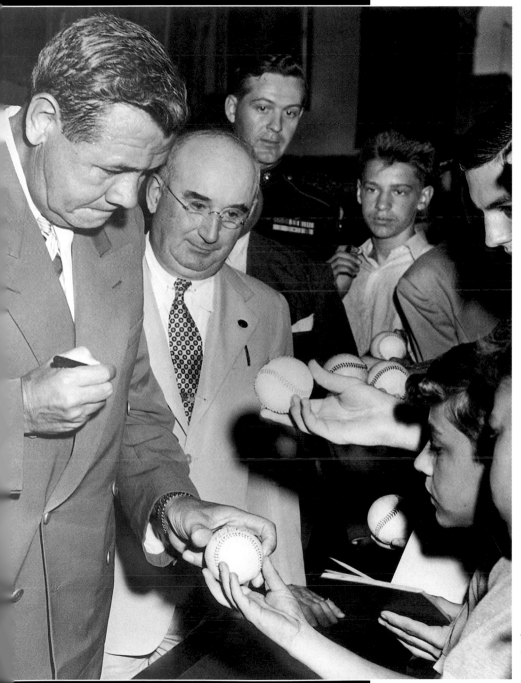

"**H**is is the biggest autograph that is wanted by everyone who collects . . . There's none bigger; it is the most cherished item in any collector's wish list."

—Barry Halper, *famous collector, in* Outside the Lines: Babe Ruth's Larger Than Life Legacy, *ESPN Documentary, 1998*

Wherever he went he took time to sign autographs.

"He revolutionized so many things about professional sports. Ruth was the first superstar. All of us should feel a great deal of thanks for what he did for all of us."

—WAYNE GRETSKY, *NHL, in* Outside the Lines: Babe Ruth's Larger Than Life Legacy, *ESPN Documentary, 1998*

◆　◆　◆

"The name helped—Babe Ruth—I mean see if his name was Harold Thompson it wouldn't have the same impact. Italian immigrants called him "Bambino." The Bam hits one—everything fit—you didn't forget him, he was indelible. Everyone who saw him had a story—remembered something about him. Every place he went he sort of left a trail."

—ROBERT W. CREAMER, *quoted in* Babe Ruth, *HBO Documentary, 1998*

◆　◆　◆

"Babe Ruth was the eighteen carat center of the golden age. He was a huge, good-natured lummox who called everybody "Kid" or "Joe" because he couldn't remember their real names. He had an incredible flamboyance, with the talent to back it up. Some of the players resented him. He was a one-man gang who didn't pay much attention to anybody else's feelings. He was also getting more money than anybody else in baseball, and more than twice as much as anybody on the Yankees. But he was worth every penny of it. He brought in two dollars through the turnstiles for every dollar Ruppert paid him."

—ELEANOR GEHRIG, *(Lou Gehrig's wife) quoted in Joseph Durso,* DiMaggio: The Last American Knight, *1995*

Inhibited? Never!
Babe was always
ready for the next
"act."

87

"The season of 1921 was also the one in which I acquired my manager, Christy Walsh, who made a lot of money for me as I did for him. But I'll always be grateful for what Christy did for me. Christy is a persistent guy who just won't take no for an answer. In fact, that's how he became my manager.

"When I knocked out those 54 homers in 1920 I got all kinds of outside offers. People wanted me to endorse everything from suspenders to wallpaper. We never knew what was sound or wildcat.

"I always liked people and never was a difficult guy to see. But by 1921 they had me plain nuts. They'd camp on the doorstep of the apartment house in which I then lived in Washington Heights, back of the Polo Grounds, and I used to have to sneak in through the janitor's entrance to get to my own apartment. I'd put in a private, unlisted phone and a couple of weeks later all kinds of strangers would have my number.

"Christy took charge of all my outside earnings. I'd growl at him now and then, and occasionally would want to wring his neck when he'd put my money where I couldn't reach it, for I was always a fellow who could spend it faster than I could make it. During my first year under Christy's management my newspaper earnings alone jumped from less than $500 to $15,000. And that was only one sideline he improved for me."

—BABE RUTH, *as told to Bob Considine,* The Babe Ruth Story, *1948*
(Christy Walsh is considered the first sports agent.)

Daydreaming about Babe Ruth, talking about Babe Ruth and writing about Babe Ruth has absorbed a lot of other people's time. This spindle-legged, pot bellied, throwaway man-child not only became the Sultan of Swat for baseball fans, he appealed also to everyday Americans caught in changing times. Here was a man who not only embraced the greedy new consumerism of the twenties, but also evoked nostalgic longings for a less complicated society where traditional value ruled.

—ROBERT LIPSYTE AND PETER LEVINE,
Idols of the Game, *1995*

Babe Ruth and Old Jack Dempsey
Both Sultans of the Swat
One hits where other people are—
The other where they're not.

—JOHN LARDNER, *quoted in Franklin P. Adams,*
The Diary of Our Own Samuel Pepys

◆　◆　◆

I was with Babe one evening when he turned down a one-way street—the wrong way.

"This is a one-way street," said the cop.

"I'm only driving one way!" yelled Ruth.

"Oh, hello Babe! I didn't know it was you," replied the cop. "Go anywhere you please, but take it easy!"

And so it went.

—GRANTLAND RICE, *sportswriter and author,*
The Tumult and the Shouting, *1954*

Lou Gehrig and Babe at Dexter Park in Brooklyn, New York, October 1928, advertising a rodeo that was coming to Madison Square Garden

Roistering was a way of life, yet Ruth was no boozer. Three drinks of hard liquor left him fuzzy. He could consume great quantities of beer, he was a prodigious eater and his prowess with women was legendary. Sleep was something he got when other appetites were sated. He arose when he chose and almost invariably was the last to arrive in the clubhouse where Doc Woods, the Yankee trainer, always had bicarbonate soda ready. Before a change in clothes, the Babe would measure out a mound of bicarb smaller than the pyramid Cheops, mix and gulp it down. Then Jim Kahn says, "He would belch and all the loose water in the showers would fall down."

—RED SMITH, *author and columnist,* The Red Smith Reader, *1982*

As he made and spent money he tried to pick up social graces, sometimes with hilarious results. Particularly later on after he joined the Yankees and began to live in New York, where he was inevitably drawn into the social world.

He once accompanied Ford Frick [National League President] to a formal dinner party. Frick said that Babe would always move slowly at first when he was at affairs of this sort, watching, noting, finding out how you did things before doing them himself. A rather splendid asparagus salad was served. Babe's eyes sidled around until he saw which fork was to be used. He casually lifted the fork, poked at the salad and then without touching it put the fork down and pushed the plate away.

"Don't you care for the salad, Mr. Ruth?" his hostess asked.

"Oh, it's not that," he replied, his voice elegant and unctuous. "It's just that asparagus makes my urine smell."

—ROBERT W. CREAMER, Babe: The Legend Comes to Life, *1974*

"If Babe were alive today I get the feeling he'd still be a big fan favorite. He'd still love kids. He'd still love playing the game. He'd still get a thrill out of people asking for his autograph and he'd still take the time to give it to them."

—GREG SCHWALENBERG, *curator, The Babe Ruth Birthplace Museum , 2000*

For the first time, Claire (Hodgson) Ruth watched from a box near the dugout. Naturally, the bridegroom hit a home run. Rounding the bases, he halted at second and swept off his cap in a courtly bow to his bride. This was typical of him.

—RED SMITH, *author and columnist,* The Red Smith Reader, *1982,*
referring to the day after Ruth got married.

◆ ◆ ◆

"Who has ever looked like him since Babe Ruth? Try to think of someone who looked like him. It's like he was created for this role that he was given, and he played it to the hills."

—BILL GLEASON, *quoted in* Babe Ruth, *HBO Documentary, 1998*

◆ ◆ ◆

"As he moved, center stage moved with him."

—ROGER KAHN, *quoted in William Humber,* Let's Play Ball

"Babe was terrible at remembering names and faces. One day Lazzeri decided to have a little fun with him. He introduced Miles Thomas to the Babe as a new relief pitcher for the Yankees. Miles had actually been with the Yankees for 3 or 4 years as a pitcher, but when Lazzeri introduced Thomas to Ruth, he said, 'Nice to see ya keed, welcome to the Yankees.'"

—ROBERT W. CREAMER, *quoted in* Babe Ruth, *HBO Documentary, 1998*

"But the best of them all [ballparks] is the Polo Grounds. Boy, how I used to sock 'em in there. I cried when they took me out of the Polo Grounds." [While playing his home games in the Polo Grounds in 1920 and 1921, Ruth had hit fifty-four and fifty-nine home runs.]

—BABE RUTH, *as told to Frank Graham*, New York Sun

"Some twenty years ago, I stopped talking about the Babe for the simple reason that I realized that those who had never seen him didn't believe me."

—TOMMY HOLMES, *sportswriter, quoted in John Tullius,* I'd Rather Be a Yankee, *1986*

MORE BITS ON THE BAMBINO

- Over his career with the Yankees, Babe's salary rose from $20,000 in 1920 to $80,000 in 1930–31.

- The Giants had always been the top draw in New York until Ruth arrived in 1920. Then suddenly the crowds at the Polo Grounds grew larger for the Yankees than the Giants. The Yankees doubled their home attendance from 1919–20; they drew 1,289,422 in 1920—the first team ever to break the million mark. (The Yankees played at the Polo Grounds until Yankee Stadium was built in 1923.)

- To see Babe play, it cost 55 cents for a bleacher seat and $2.20 for the finest, closest box seat.

- According to CMG Worldwide, the official licensing and representation firm for Babe Ruth, the Bambino is the number-one deceased sports personality in licensing and marketing today. He has over 400 licensed products.

- It is estimated Ruth made about $500,000 in outside money over his career, big money, particularly during the Depression.

Baseball was Babe's first passion, golf was his second.

◆ Babe's favorite pastimes were playing golf and bridge. Golf was perhaps his favorite . . . in fact he was playing golf in California when the deal was made that sent him from Boston to New York. The deal became final on December 26, 1919, and Miller Huggins, the Yankee manager, was sent to California to tell Babe prior to the public announcement on January 5, 1920.

◆ Babe was married twice. First to Helen Woodford on October 14, 1914, when she was seventeen and Babe was nineteen. In 1921, they adopted an infant daughter, Dorothy, who was rumored to be Babe's legitimate child out of wedlock. Helen and Babe were legally married for fifteen years, but separated after 1925. Helen died on January 11, 1929, of suffocation due to a fire. She was thirty one. On April 17, 1929, he married his girlfriend Claire Hodgson. Claire had a daughter, Julia, from a previous marriage. In October 1930, Claire and Babe legally adopted each other's daughters.

◆ Babe had one sister, Mamie, who lived in Hagerstown, Maryland. Mamie died at the age of ninety-one in July 1992.

◆ The phrase "The Babe Ruth of . . ." or "Ruthian" is commonly used to refer to someone or something at the very top. "Ruthian" is the standard by which great accomplishments are measured—the very pinnacle of success.

Claire and Babe on vacation. Babe always looked dapper—note his matching shoes and swimsuit.

◆ As an actor, Ruth played himself in the movie biography of Lou Gehrig, *The Pride of the Yankees*. Joining Ruth, also playing themselves, were former Yankees Bill Dickey, Bob Meusel, and Mark Koenig, as well as Bill Stein, the sportscaster.

◆ The Babe was utterly indifferent to names. To him, any male regardless of age was "keed," a young woman was "sister," and an elderly woman, "mother."

The Ruth family: Dorothy, Claire, Babe, and Julia

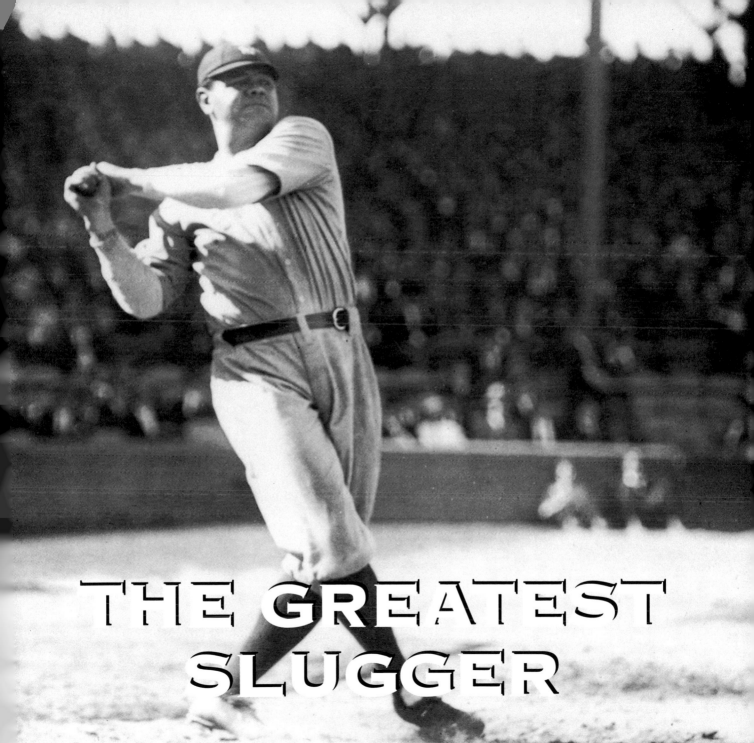

> ## "It's almost as if when anybody hits a home run today they should pay Babe Ruth a royalty. It's like he invented it."
>
> —DONALD HONIG, *sportswriter, in* Outside the Lines: Babe Ruth's
> Larger Than Life Legacy, *ESPN Documentary, 1998*

Babe was a fully crafted slugger. His body, bat, balance, and brain came together with precision timing to create his massive swing. If he so much as made contact with the ball, there was a good chance his mighty blast would leave the stadium. Nothing could electrify a crowd more than that definitive sound of the ball taking off. Never having had the benefit of strength and conditioning coaches, weight rooms, or indoor batting cages, Babe had more raw power than most current sluggers and played in much larger parks.

Babe's first major league home run came as a Boston Red Sox, on May 6, 1915, against Jack Warhop of the Yankees. In 1920, his first season with the Yankees, Babe's first home run, ironically, was off Herb Pennock of the Boston Red Sox, on May 1, 1920. It was his fiftieth career homer.

Babe, a left-handed hitter, became the first player to hit thirty home runs, then forty, then fifty, then sixty. He hit fifty twice before anyone else hit thirty. He proceeded to hit thirty or more in a total of thirteen seasons, forty or more in eleven seasons, and fifty or more in four different seasons. In 1920, he out-homered every team in the American League. Between 1926 and 1931, Ruth had six straight seasons in which he hit forty-six or more home runs.

Ruth was not only recognized for the number of home runs but also for the distance they soared. Babe set distance records in virtually every stadium in which he played and hit at least one five-hundred-foot home run in each of the eight American League parks in 1921 alone.

When he led the American League with fifty-four home runs in 1920, the runner-up had just nineteen. In 1921, when he led the league with fifty-nine, the runner-up had only twenty-four. In all, he led the league in home runs a dozen times. His last home run, Number 714, was on May 25, 1935, in Pittsburgh as a Boston Brave.

◆　◆　◆

The home run, an occasional offensive phenomenon when a team hit a total of twenty in a season, came to be regarded as the ultimate offensive weapon.

—RED SMITH, *author and columnist*, The Red Smith Reader, *1982*

"For Babe to smash the first home run, how could it be otherwise."

—Bob Elson, *Chicago White Sox announcer, commenting on Babe's home run in the first All-Star Game on July 6, 1933, played at Comiskey Park, quoted in Curt Smith,* Voices of the Game

◆   ◆   ◆

"There's forty thousand people here who know that last one was a ball, tomato head." [Babe arguing after being called out on strikes.] "Maybe so, but mine is the only opinion that counts."

Babe Tinelli, *umpire, quoted in* George F. Will, Men at Work: The Craft of Baseball, *1990*

◆   ◆   ◆

The Babe always thought he was the best home run hitter. He wanted to be the best. If he had known someone [Roger Maris] was going to break his record of 60 in a season, he would have hit 70. If he had known that some day someone [Hank Aaron] was going to break 714, he would have hit 800."

—Dick Reese, *quoted by Dick Miller in the* Sporting News, *August 4, 1973*

◆   ◆   ◆

It wasn't just that he hit more home runs than anybody else, he hit them better, higher, farther, with more theatrical timing and a more flamboyant flourish. Nobody could strike out like Babe Ruth. Nobody circled the bases with the same pigeon-toed, mincing majesty.

—Red Smith, *author and columnist,* The Red Smith Reader, *1982*

"I may be a pitcher, but first off I'm a hitter. I copied my swing after Joe Jackson's. His is the perfect test. Joe aims his right shoulder square at the pitcher, with his feet about twenty inches apart. But I close my stance to about eight and a half inches or less. I find I pivot better with it closed. Once committed . . . once my swing starts, though, I can't change it or pull up. It's all or nothing at all."

—BABE RUTH, *quoted in Grantland Rice,* The Tumult and the Shouting, *1954*

Babe portraying a young slugger in the 1920s silent film *Headin' Home*

101

"By 1918 Ruth's slugging, not his pitching, was the talk of the American League. The war had decreased the pool of players available so that many of those remaining were pressed into service at more than one position, and Ruth began to play in the outfield. He promptly hit eleven homers for the Red Sox, tying Tilly Walker of the Athletics for the home-run title. In 1919, before the Black Sox Series played itself out, Ruth hit twenty-nine out of the park, for his first home-run title. Gavvy Cravath of the Phillies, in the National League, hit only twelve the same year, but managed to top his league. Wally Pipp led the American League in homers with twelve in 1916, and again in 1917 with nine. Such numbers were picayune in comparison to the explosions about to erupt off Ruth's bat, and he would go on to revolutionize baseball."

—LOU GEHRIG, *New York Yankee first baseman, 1923–39, quoted in Ray Robinson,*
Iron Horse: Lou Gehrig in His Time, *1990*

◆　　◆　　◆

"John McGraw was the best inside baseball manager. He perfected the Baltimore chop, bunt, move the runner along, work for one run at a time. Then this guy [Ruth] came along and broke up ball games with one swing. He [McGraw] hated him. For 30 years he worked for one run, and Babe wrecked the whole afternoon with one swipe."

—JOHN KENNELLY, *broadcaster, in* Babe Ruth, *HBO Documentary, 1998*

"The power wasn't only in Ruth's bat. I remember when Joe McCarthy took over as manager. Ruth had been getting about 150 walks a year with Tony Lazzeri hitting behind him most of the time.

"I heard him walk up to McCarthy and say, 'I'll tell you how to make the lineup. I'm going to bat third and I want [Lou] Gehrig behind me. You can fill the other seven spots.'

"McCarthy said, 'That's fine with me, Babe.'"

—DICK REESE, *quoted by Dick Miller in the* Sporting News, *August 4, 1973*

Ruth said before the game that he felt a home run coming on and refused to participate in batting practice. "I have an idea," he said, "that I'm about to sock one and I'm not going to waste any time hitting 'em now when they don't count.

—RUD RENNIE, New York Herald-Tribune, *June 1927*

◆ ◆ ◆

Today, other men have hit more home runs, both in a single season and throughout an entire career. The years are littered with those who have been faster or stronger. Yet no performer—and make no mistake; that's exactly what Babe Ruth was—ever cast a longer or more durable shadow across the Republic.

—MIKE BARNICLE, ESPN the Magazine, *September 14, 1999*

In 1920 Babe Ruth took New York by storm. He hit an unbelievable 54 home runs in his first year in the Big Apple, to shatter his record of 29 the previous year. That was 35 more than the second best total that year of 19, by the great George Sisler. Everyone else's hitting looked puny next to the colossal clouts of the Babe.

—JOHN TULLIUS, I'd Rather Be a Yankee, *1986*

◆　　◆　　◆

"The home run became glorified with Babe Ruth. Starting with him, batters have been thinking in terms of how far they could hit the ball, not how often."

—ROGERS HORNSBY, *St. Louis Cardinal player, quoted in Paul Dickson,*
Baseball's Greatest Quotations, *1992*

◆　　◆　　◆

"He was very brave at the plate. You rarely saw him fall away from a pitch. He stayed right in there. No one drove him out."

—CASEY STENGEL, *New York Yankee manager, 1949–60 quoted in*
Robert W. Creamer, Babe: The Legend Comes to Life

Frames of his famous swing

"The most striking thing about Ruth at bat was not simply the power that he generated but also the beauty of his swing. He made home run hitting look so easy. There was no violence in his stroke. He put everything into it, but he never looked like he was extending himself. By the time he hit the ball, he had taken a long stride forward and had turned his shoulders and ass and wrists into it, swinging through it. Exquisite timing. I can close my eyes and not only see the swing but still admire it."

—SHIRLEY POVICH, Washington Post *sportswriter,*
quoted in "Babe Ruth," Sports Illustrated,
September 1998

The bigger the crowd, the bigger the Babe. It was only natural therefore that some of his greatest achievements, such as the home run against Root, should come in World Series competition. Ruth was a money player and had the true star's ability to rise to the situation. He made all sorts of plays in his Series career, brilliant in all of them save the 1922 flopperoo against the Giants. In his last five World Series, of which the Yankees won four, the big fellow hit a total of fourteen home runs.

—TOM MEANY, Babe Ruth: The Big Moments and the Big Fella, *1947*

◆　　◆　　◆

"Every time you faced him you get butterflies . . . wouldn't stop floppin' around . . . you'd think you'd get over it, but you don't . . ."

—WILLIS HUDLIN, *Cleveland Indian pitcher, 1926–40, in* Outside the Lines: Babe Ruth's Larger Than Life Legacy, *ESPN Documentary, 1998*

When he struck out, as he often did, it was with the panache of a Shakespearean actor, and he was applauded to the echo as his bat lashed the air unmercifully. Who ever heard of a baseball player striking out to the accompaniment of cheers?"

—*"Preface: A Letter from Lou,"* Ray Robinson, Iron Horse: Lou Gehrig in His Time, *1990*

Babe's famous
full circle "twist"
after a strike

But maybe most of all there is this: Home runs could be too much of a good thing. They come at a rate of one in every 30 major league at-bats now; in Ruth's heyday they came at a rate of every 91 at-bats.

—ERIK BRADY, *"Some Lament, It's Not Baseball; It's Just Powerball,"* USA Today, *August 6, 1999*

Anyone skeptical of the drawing power of George Herman Ruth must have been convinced yesterday. The presence of the mighty slugger and his pace-setting colleagues was sufficient to lure 35,000 customers into the rebuilt stands of Comiskey Park. Ruth failed to live up to his reputation as a home run hitter, but in batting practice the Bambino lifted a ball clear of the second tier of bleachers in right field. The crowd cheered. The architects had said that no one could ever hit a ball out of the park. But they hadn't counted on Mr. Ruth.

—Chicago Tribune, *May 8, 1927*

Babe's forceful follow-through

The 1927 Yankees have been picked by most experts as the greatest team of all time. By any yardstick there are some very persuasive arguments to back that claim. They were the only team in the first century of baseball who went wire to wire in first place to win the pennant. (Only the 1984 Detroit Tigers have matched that feat.) The Yankees won 110 games, a record at that time, to finish a whopping 19 games ahead of second-place Philadelphia, another record. They had already clinched the pennant by Labor Day, when they led by 24 games with 23 to play, also a record.

—JOHN TULLIUS, I'd Rather Be a Yankee, *1986*

Safe at home, August 14, 1934, scoring from second. This was Babe's last year playing for the Yankees.

Ruth became baseball's career home run hitter in 1921, which was just his third season as a full-time (non-pitching) player. He proceeded to break his own record 577 times. When in 1934 he hit his 700th home run, only two other players had more than 300. When he retired, his total of 714 was nearly twice the total of the man in second place (Gehrig, then at 378). Over a six season span (1926–1931), Ruth averaged 50 home runs, 154 RBIs, 147 runs and a .354 average.

—GEORGE F. WILL, Men at Work: The Craft of Baseball, *1990*

"I don't recall the first home run he hit off me that day. But I'll never forget the second one. He got hold of that ball and hit it clear out of the ballpark. It was the longest cockeyed ball I ever saw in my life. That poor fellow, he'd gotten to where he could hardly hobble along. When he rounded third base, I looked over there at him and he kind of looked at me. I tipped my cap, sort of to say, I've seen everything now, Babe. He looked at me and kind of saluted and smiled. We got in that gesture of good friendship. And that's the last home run he ever hit."

—GUY BUSH, *Pittsburgh Pirate pitcher, 1935–36, quoted in Lawrence S. Ritter and Mark Rucker,*
The Babe: The Game That Ruth Built, *1994*

BABE'S BAT

Babe's Hillerich Bradsby Louisville Slugger Model was thirty-five inches long and was made from hickory or northern white ash. Weighing forty-two to fifty-four ounces, it was much heavier than any of the bats used today.

Other players referred to Babe's bat as the "monstrous weapon." Today players use a lighter version weighing 33 to 34 ounces. By comparison, Mark McGuire's bat weighs thirty-three ounces. Bat speed has always been important but in Ruth's time it was thought the bigger the barrel, the bigger the fly.

"Babe Ruth hit two more homers yesterday, one of them so long that Luke Sewell, the Indians catcher, demanded an inspection of Ruth's bat.

'Lemme see that club,' demanded Mr. Sewell, after Mr. Herman had hit that ball into the center-field bleachers in front of the scoreboard. 'Lemme see that stick. Nobody could hit one like that without having a slug of lead or something in the end of his bat.'

"Mr. Sewell took the Ruth bludgeon and peered at it suspiciously. He scrutinized the end of it, balanced it in one hand, and even sniffed at the unoffensive shillalah. Though he found nothing illegal, Mr. Sewell was still dubious and unconvinced and he shook his head skeptically."

—JAMES R. HARRISON, New York Times, *June 12, 1927,*
quoted in G. H. Fleming, Murderers' Row, 1985

At last George Herman Ruth has done it. He has broken a ball with the force of his blow.

Before the second game yesterday, with Mike Gazella pitching, the Babe caught one on the end of his bat. So terrific was his swing that he broke the horsehide cover for a space of more than two inches, or half the circumference of the ball.

The broken ball is now carefully cached away in John Shibe's office as mute testimony of the force of a Ruthian swing.

—New York Evening Journal, *May 31, 1998*

◆   ◆   ◆

"I can't think of too many guys in the big league who could swing this bat and have a lot of success with it. It's top heavy so you've got to have strong hands to be able to get the barrel through the zone. My hands aren't strong enough—I can tell you that."

—Tony Gwynn, *San Diego Padre slugger, in* Outside the Lines: Babe Ruth's Larger Than Life Legacy, *ESPN Documentary, 1998*

112

"I can't use anything that big . . . Too large for me."

—Ken Griffey Jr., *then Seattle Mariner center fielder, commenting on Babe's bat, in* Outside the Lines: Babe Ruth's Larger Than Life Legacy, *ESPN Documentary, 1998 (Griffey now plays for the Cincinnati Reds.)*

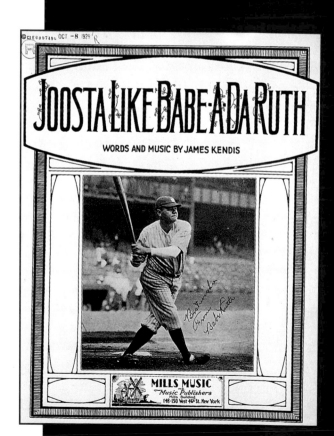

BREAKING DOWN BABE'S LIFETIME TOTAL 714 HOME RUNS

- 686 as a right fielder
- 15 as a pitcher
- 13 as a first baseman
- 49 hit with the Red Sox in 1915–19
- 659 hit with the Yankees in 1920–34
- 6 hit with the Boston Braves in 1935

- 76 hit in the Polo Grounds
- 347 hit in Yankee Stadium
- 367 hit on the road
- 499 hit against right-handed pitchers
- 215 hit against left-handed pitchers

- Number 500 was hit off Willis Hudlin of the Cleveland Indians on August 11, 1929.
- Number 600 was hit off of George Blacholder of the St. Louis Browns on August 21, 1931.
- Number 700 was hit off Tommy Bridges of the Detroit Tigers on July 13, 1934. Babe was 39 years old.
- Number 708 (last as an American Leaguer) was hit off Syd Cohen of the Washington Senators on September 29, 1934.

◆ Number 712 was hit off Red Lucas of the Pittsburgh Pirates on May 25, 1935.

◆ Numbers 713 and 714 were hit off Guy Bush of the Pittsburgh Pirates on May 25, 1935.

MORE SLUGGING FEATS

◆ On average, Babe hit a home run for every 11.8 times at bat.

◆ The sixty home runs he hit in 1927 represented 14 percent of the American League total (439). To do that today a player would have to hit more than three hundred home runs.

◆ In 1920 his slugging percentage was .847 and in 1921 it was .846. No other player has ever reached .800.

◆ Babe led the American League in home runs twelve times and in RBIs six times.

◆ Babe hit .422 in opening-day games—five doubles, one triple, and seven home runs.

◆ Two hundred sixteen pitchers surrendered home runs to Babe, coincidentally Babe was born at 216 Emory Street.

◆ Babe was on ten World Series teams and won the title four times. In 1923, the first year the Yankees ever won the World Series, they beat the New York Giants, their crosstown rivals, four games to two. The 1927, 1928, and 1932 titles were won in sweeps. In 1927 the Yankees swept the Pittsburgh Pirates, in 1928 it was the St. Louis Cardinals, and in 1932, the Chicago Cubs. The 1927 and 1928 sweeps were the first back to back by the same team.

◆ In forty-one World Series games, thirty-six of them with the Yankees, Ruth hit .326 with fifteen homers, thirty-three RBIs and thirty-seven runs scored. In his seven Series with the Yankees, Ruth hit .300 or better, except in 1922.

◆ Babe was one of only two players (Reggie Jackson being the other in 1977) to ever hit three home runs in a World Series game, and is the only one to do it twice (1926 and 1928). He also hit three home runs in a single game twice in regular season play. His last three home runs, Numbers 712, 713, and 714, were hit in the same game on May 25, 1935.

◆ The first All-Star Game was played on July 6, 1933, in Chicago. Always primed for the drama of an important moment, Ruth hit the first All-Star home run in the third inning, a two-run shot off pitcher Bill Hallahan that provided the American League's margin in a 4–3 victory. Babe Ruth was named the Most Valuable Player of the game. The All-Star Game was the idea of Arch Ward, the sports editor of the *Chicago Tribune*. The best players from each league would play each other as the featured sports event of the Chicago Century of Progress Exposition. A box seat cost $1.65 a grandstand seat $1.10 and a bleacher ticket 55 cents.

◆ Babe set a major league record for the number of times he hit two or more home runs in one game during the regular season: seventy-two. He accomplished this feat four times in World Series play for a total of seventy-six double homer games.

◆ Ruth played before the era of the tape-measure home run, which means every long hit is carefully computed to the inch. None of Ruth's towering smashes were ever officially measured, but the best guess of his longest is 550 feet.

◆ The right-field bleacher section at Yankee Stadium was called Ruthville. He hit most of his home runs to that section. Many baseball authorities have stated that the foul pole was invented mainly for him to gauge his swing.

◆ Babe was a charter member of the National Baseball Hall of Fame when it opened in 1936. The four other players inducted with Babe were Ty Cobb, Walter Johnson, Christy Mathewson, and Honus Wagner.

Mementos from St. Mary's Industrial School for Boys where Babe lived for most of his boyhood

Babe Ruth's rookie card (1914)

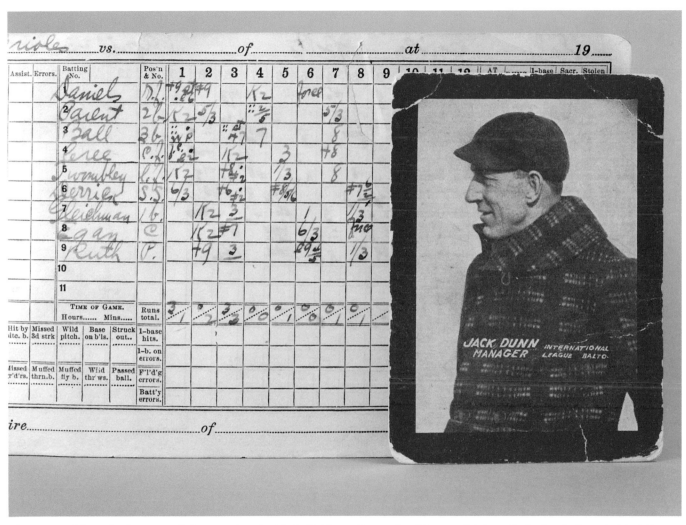

The scorecard from the first game Babe ever played with the Baltimore International League Orioles with the baseball card of Jack Dunn, the owner and manager of the team (1914)

Babe (center) and his father, George Herman Ruth (right), at the family saloon on the corner of Eutaw and Lombard Streets, in Baltimore. The inscription on the bottle reads "George Ruth proprietor."

A pinup of Babe with some of his equipment. "Ruth" is embroidered on the inside of his New York Yankee uniform pants.

left: Statues of Babe. He was a favorite subject of artists. Left, stained glass by John Redfern, 1998. Center, plaster on a wood base by Henry Berge, 1958. Right, bronze by Palmer Murphy, 1994.

below: Official team payroll check signed by Yankee owner Jacob Ruppert (1925)

THE AMERICAN LEAGUE BASE BALL CLUB
OF NEW YORK, INC.

No. 8458

NEW YORK, SEP 1 1925 192___

PAY TO THE ORDER OF _____ GEORGE H. RUTH _____ $ 4598.84

THE SUM OF $4598 AND 84 CTS _____ **DOLLARS**

TO **YORKVILLE BANK**
1511 THIRD AVE.
NEW YORK.

Jacob Ruppert

PRESIDENT.

Because of Babe's popularity he was featured on many covers, from *Vanity Fair* to *Popular Science*.

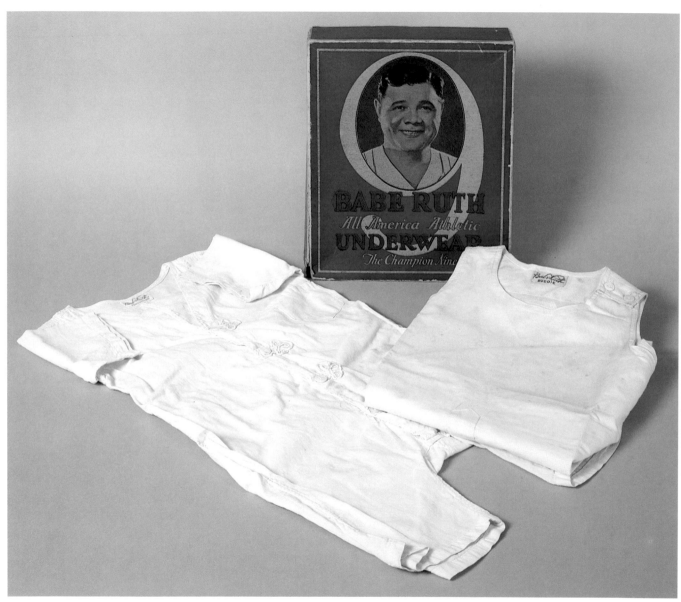

Babe was one of the nation's most powerful product endorsers.

His name and image appeared on hundreds of commercial items, including cereal boxes, candy bar wrappers, watches, and buttons.

Babe in bronze—a very realistic likeness. By Armand LaMontagne, 1996.

Yankee sweater and autographed balls. Julia Ruth Stevens, Mrs. Babe Ruth, Babe Ruth.

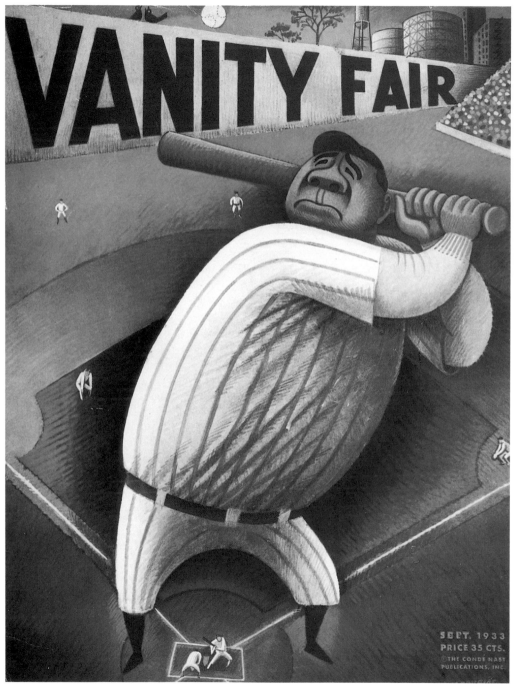

Caricature of Babe on the cover of *Vanity Fair,* September 1933

The trunk Babe took
to Japan in 1934 for
the All-American
All-Stars barnstorming
tour

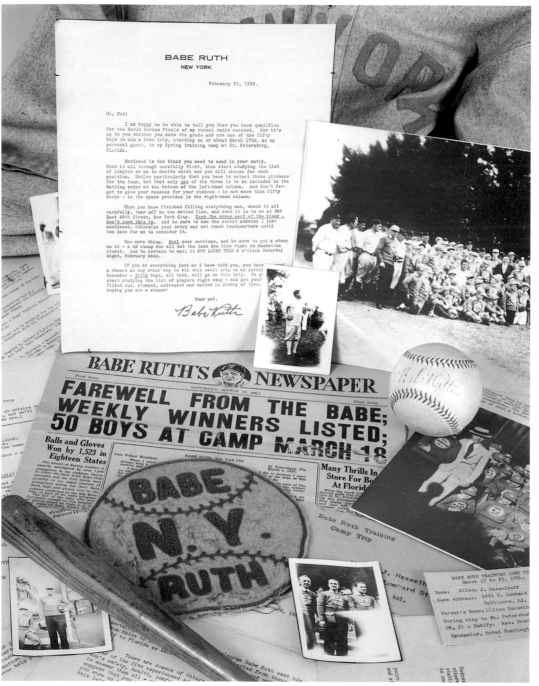

From a radio contest in which fifty boys were selected to be Babe's guests at spring training in 1934. The letter is telling them that they have qualified for the finals to win the free trip. Photo on top is Babe and the winners.

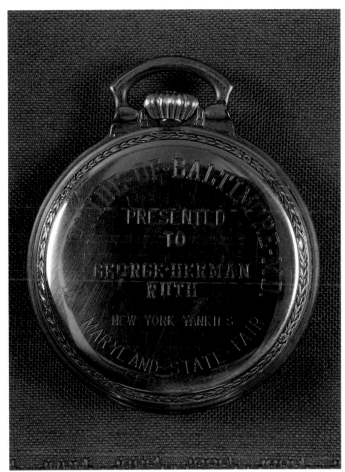

Inscription on watch reads "The Pride of Baltimore, Maryland.
Presented to George Herman Ruth, New York Yankees,
Maryland State Fair, September 1927."

This official American League ball may be the very last one Babe ever signed. The original mailing box pictured here gives New York's Memorial Hospital as the return address, dated August 18, 1948. Babe died the next day.

A FORCE
IN THE FIELD

> How many times do runners try to make two bases on a single to right field on Ruth. Not often, unless the hit and run play is on and the base runner has a long lead. Ruth is a good hitter, but he has never been given enough credit for his fielding ability. Few fielders cover more ground than Ruth.
>
> —FRED LIEB, New York Post, *August 15, 1927*

Just as he made slugging home runs look easy, Babe made playing the outfield look effortless as well. Although he ran with short mincing strides, he was quick, and chased after fly balls with eagerness, often leaping and lunging to make the catch. Babe rarely made an error in the field and his keen anticipation and strong throwing arm often cut off extra-base hits. While his reputation as a hitter overshadowed his prowess in the field, throughout his career he regularly made big defensive plays.

Although Babe Ruth is generally known as a right fielder—his position in Yankee Stadium—he actually played left field in the majority of ballparks.

What many people don't realize about the Babe is that he was a fantastic all-around athlete, with natural talent and natural instincts. When I broke in with the Tigers in 1933, Babe was playing left field. One day a guy hit a long fly to left with a man on second base. Babe went back to the wall, stopped, turned around, and looked, as if the ball was going out of the park. At the last second, Babe turned and caught the ball. Then he threw to second and caught the runner for a double play. What timing! I never saw anything like that before, but Babe had been playing for twenty years. In his prime he could do anything. He could pitch, he could steal bases, he could throw, he could run, he could hit, and he could win.

—HANK GREENBERG, *Detroit Tiger first baseman, 1930, 1933–41,* The Story of My Life

A spring training feat with the New York Yankees

The Babe roamed into the right field corner yesterday and chucked out Johnny Bassler trying to stretch a single. The Babe throws out a lot of 'em trying to stretch singles.

—W. B. HANNA, New York Herald-Tribune, *September 26, 1927*

"I never realized until this season what a really good player he is. I had regarded Ruth only as a phenomenal hitter. Now I know he deserves to be rated among the greatest outfielders of all time. He covers a wide territory, is sure death on fly balls and all the line drives he can get his hands on, plays ground balls that come to him as well as an infielder, and throws amazingly. I have seen a lot of accurate throwing by outfielders, but I never saw a man who had a slight edge on the Babe in pegging. (Sometimes during fielding practice a towel would be laid down near home plate, and from deep right field Babe Ruth would throw in baseballs that more often than not would hit the towel.)"

—ARTHUR FLETCHER, *New York Yankee third-base coach, 1926–45,*
quoted by Frank Graham, New York Sun, *May 25, 1927,*
quoted in G. H. Fleming, Murderers' Row, *1985*

He was an accomplished outfielder with astonishing range for his bulk, a powerful arm and keen baseball sense. It was said that he never made a mental error.

—RED SMITH, *author and columnist*,
The Red Smith Reader, *1982*

Clowning around with a
happy young fan

"There was only one Babe Ruth. He went on the ball field like he was playing in a cow pasture, with cows for an audience. He never knew what fear or nervousness was. He played by instinct, sheer instinct. He wasn't smart, he didn't have any education, but he never made a wrong move on the ball field.

"One of the greatest pitchers of all time, and then he became a great judge of the fly ball. Never threw to the wrong base when he was playing the outfield, terrific arm, good base runner, could hit the ball twice as far as any other human being. He was like a damn animal. He had that instinct. They know when it's going to rain, things like that. Nature—that was Ruth."

—RUBE BRESSLER, *third baseman, Cincinnati Reds, 1917–29, and Brooklyn Dodgers , 1927–32, quoted in Lawrence S. Ritter,* The Glory of Their Times, *1984*

◆ ◆ ◆

Ruth looked pretty good going after Harry Rice's liner in the fifth. The ball looked as if it was bound for China when the Babe caught up with it [in left-center field] took it in his bare hand on the first bounce, and held Harry to two bases.

—RUD RENNIE, New York Herald-Tribune, *May 13, 1927*

THE HISTORIC 60TH HOME RUN

September 30, 1927—Creating the single-season
record that stood for thirty-four years

They could no more have stopped Babe Ruth from hitting the home run that gave him a new record than you could halt a locomotive by sticking your foot out. Once he had 59, 60 was as sure as the rising sun.

—PAUL GALLICO, New York Daily News, *October 1, 1927*

In 1927, Babe Ruth and Lou Gehrig, the most popular tandem in American sports, were engaged in a back and forth home run battle that can be compared to the Mark McGwire and Sammy Sosa duels of 1998 and 1999.

Some of the differences between then and now were that Ruth and Gehrig were teammates—Ruth batted third and Gehrig fourth—there was no television, no night games, the equipment was heavier, and players wore wool uniforms—very hot for the humid days of summer.

The excitement that summer was unbelievable . . . their battle captured headlines daily. This was the first time anyone had directly challenged Ruth. On July 5, Gehrig's home runs totaled twenty-eight to Ruth's twenty-five. By August 25, Ruth had forty to Gehrig's thirty-nine, and on September 6 they were tied at forty-four. But it was in September that Ruth pulled away, walloping seventeen and winding up with sixty to Gehrig's forty-seven.

Ruth's sixtieth was hit before the hometown crowd at Yankee Stadium in a game against the Washington Senators. He beat his own record of fifty-nine hit in 1921 at the Polo Grounds (the Yankees' previous home field). These sixty home runs were four more than any other team had that year, except the Yankees.

The 1927 Yankees rank as one of the greatest teams of all time. They were the first team to go wire to wire in first place to win the pennant with a nineteen game lead over Philadelphia—the biggest margin in history. The Yankees won 110 games, also a record and set another record with 158 home runs and went on to sweep the Pittsburgh Pirates in the World Series.

Babe and Lou: back to back in the lineup; side by side in the dugout

"I was pitching my best. After I served him four balls in the first inning, I said to myself, 'Well, Babe, if you want to hit any homers today, you'd better start swinging.' I had made up my mind I wasn't going to give him a good pitch all afternoon. The ball Babe hit for his sixtieth homer was the kind of ball no other batter would even have tried for. It was a curve ball, high, straight at him. You might call it a bean ball. The score was tied. There was one man out and one man on third. I wanted to get the Babe away from the plate. Instead of stepping back, he waded right into the ball. He lunged for it before it ever got over the plate and pulled it around into the stands. I don't see yet how he did it. He never hit a worse ball in his life. Not one that would be more difficult to hit into the stands."

—Tom Zachary, *Washington Senator pitcher, 1919–1925, off whom Babe hit his sixtieth home run, quoted in John Tullius,* I'd Rather Be a Yankee, *1986*

◆　◆　◆

"In 1927, Ruth set his home-run record of sixty and he got plenty of support from the fact that he batted number three in the lineup with Lou batting number four. Whenever Babe went to the plate, the pitcher had two possibilities: walk him or pitch to him. If he chose to pitch, Babe might strike out—or he might knock the ball out of sight. But after Lou started to bat after him, the pitchers faced double jeopardy. If they chose to walk Ruth intentionally, they'd face Gehrig with Ruth on base. They were some pair."

—Eleanor Gehrig, *Lou Gehrig's wife, quoted in Joseph Durso,* DiMaggio: The Last American Knight, *1995*

"The 60th didn't mean that much at the time because I caught that game and I didn't remember until years later when someone mentioned it to me. We didn't have a big celebration because he was only breaking his own record. Babe never bothered about it. He figured, if I played tomorrow I might hit another. He had no one to battle."

—BENNY BENGOUGH, *New York Yankee catcher, 1923–30,*
quoted in John Tullius, I'd Rather Be a Yankee, *1986*

◆　　◆　　◆

It was hit down the right field line, just fair, and Tom Zachary, the opposing pitcher yelled, "Foul ball! Foul ball!" and argued with the umpire.

In 1947 Zachary shook hands with Ruth in Yankee Stadium, and the Babe, his voice a croak from the cancer that was killing him, said, "You crooked-arm son of a bitch, are you still claiming that ball was foul?"

—ROBERT W. CREAMER, Babe: The Legend Comes to Life, *1974*

Then the ball broke sharply, coming in a good six inches inside the plate and low, and the big fellow altered his swing, which was half way completed, to meet the change in the path of the ball. When Babe finally hit the ball, he hit it off his shoe tops and golfed it into the right field bleachers for his sixtieth home run of the season.

All of this, of course, happened in a split second, but try and realize the reactions and reflexes of Ruth and you'll have some idea of why he was the greatest home run hitter the game has ever known. Here he had started a swing, the object of which was to hit a ball which he expected to come over a corner of the plate about waist high and he had to change directions in mid-air, so to speak, to hit at a ball which was six inches inside and about ankle high.

For the average hitter it would have been a miracle to have hit the ball at all, or even to have been able to check his swing but with the big fellow he not only altered the course of his swing and met the ball, but knocked it out of the park.

—TOM MEANY, Babe Ruth: The Big Moments and the Big Fella, *1947*

In 1927 he whooped it up in the clubhouse, shouting, "Sixty, count 'em, sixty!" Let's see some other son of a bitch match that!"

—ROBERT W. CREAMER, Babe: The Legend Comes to Life, *1974*

◆　◆　◆

The ball which became Homer 60 was caught by Joe Forner of 1937 First Avenue, Manhattan. He is 40 years old and has been following baseball for 35 years. As soon as the game was over, he rushed to the dressing room to let the Babe know who had the ball.

—New York Times, *October 1, 1927*

As the mighty Babe galloped around the base paths, the stands became one tumultuous ovation. Nothing like it has been seen since the Stadium was built. It exceeded the outburst that greeted Bob Meusel's hit that made the Yanks the World Champions in 1923. It rivaled anything that Broadway has ever given a visiting celebrity. No star of the great White Way was ever acclaimed so fervently. Even the veteran newspapermen, whose calloused souls have been accustomed to such demonstrations, stopped their typewriters, rose to their feet, and applauded.

The players chorused their approval. They jumped to their feet as the ball descended among the bleacherites, and they stamped their feet and slapped each other on the back.

The final big thrill came as the Babe started for the dugout after catching Walter Johnson's fly in the ninth. Fans scaled the bleacher screen and ran after the Babe; they came from the boxes and the grandstand. And as the Babe was wending his way to the dugout, those persons, among them millionaires and newsboys, slapped him on the back. And Babe liked it.

—CHARLES SEGAR, New York Daily Mirror, *October 1, 1927*

When Babe stepped to the plate in the momentous eighth inning the score was deadlock. Koenig was on third base, the result of a triple, one man was out and all was tense. It was the Babe's fourth trip to the plate during that afternoon, a base on balls and two singles resulting on his other visits plateward.

The first Zachary offering was a fast one, which sailed over for a called strike. The next was high. The Babe took a vicious swing at the third pitched ball and the bat connected with a crack that was audible in all parts of the stand. It was not necessary to follow the course of the ball. The boys in the bleachers indicated the route of the record homer. It dropped half way to the top. No. 60 was some homer, a fitting wallop to top the Babe's record of 59 in 1921.

While the crowd cheered and the Yankee players roared their greetings the Babe made his triumphant, almost regal tour of the paths. He jogged around slowly, touched each bag firmly and carefully and when he imbedded his spike in the rubber disk to record officially Homer 60, hats were tossed into the air, papers were torn up and tossed liberally and the spirit of celebration permeated the place.

The Babe's stroll out to his position was the signal for a handkerchief salute in which all the bleacherites, to the last man, participated. Jovial Babe entered into the carnival spring and punctuated his kingly stride with a succession of snappy military salutes.

—*"Ruth Crashes 60th to Set New Record,"* New York Times, *October 1, 1927, in* The Baseball Anthology, *edited by Joseph Wallace, 1994*

Supposedly "over the hill," slipping down the steps of Time, stumbling toward the discard, six years past his peak, Babe Ruth stepped out and hung up a new record at which all the sport world may stand and wonder. What Big Bill Tilden couldn't do on the tennis court, Babe Ruth has done on the diamond. What Dempsey couldn't do with his fists, Ruth has done with his bat. He came back.

Put it in the book in letters of gold. It will be a long time before any one betters that home-run mark, and a still longer time before any aging athlete makes such a gallant and glorious charge over the come-back trail.

—JOHN KIERAN, *"Was There Ever a Guy Like Ruth?"* New York Times, *October 2, 1927*

More music for the "Master of the Swing"

131

1927 NEW YORK YANKEES
WORLD CHAMPIONS

Front Row — JULIE WERA, MIKE GAZELLA, PAT COLLINS, EDDIE BENNETT (mascot), BENNY BENGOUGH, RAY MOREHART, MYLES THOMAS, CEDRIC DURST.
Middle Row — URBAN SHOCKER, JOE DUGAN, EARLE COMBS, CHARLIE O'LEARY (Coach), MILLER HUGGINS (Manager), ART FLETCHER (Coach), MARK KOENIG, DUTCH RUETHER, JOHNNY GRABOWSKI, GEORGE PIPGRAS.
Back Row — LOU GEHRiG, HERB PENNOCK, TONY LAZZERI, WILEY MOORE, BABE RUTH, DON MILLER, BOB MEUSEL, BOB SHAWK WAITE HOYT, JOE GIARD, BEN PASCHAL, (Unknown), DOC WOOD (Trainer).

A more determined athlete than George Herman Ruth never lived. With a new record in sight he was bound to make it. Ruth is like that. He is one of the few utterly dependable news stories in sports. When the crisis arises he never fails to supply the yarn. A child of destiny is George Herman. He moves in his orbit like a planet.

—PAUL GALLICO, New York Daily News,
October 1, 1927

Considered by many baseball experts as the greatest team ever, the World Champion 1927 New York Yankees. Babe is in the last row fifth from left.

R uth set the home-run mark, whacking the famous and fabulous total of 60 round-trippers. He also managed to hit .356 even though he obviously was swinging for the fences. Gehrig grew to super stardom that year, batting .373 with 175 RBIs. He also ripped 47 home runs, more than any other man had ever hit besides Ruth. But then, who-ever said that Ruth was merely a man.

—JOHN TULLIUS, *I'd Rather Be a Yankee*, *1986*

◆ ◆ ◆

1927 **became Ruth's year, the enduring symbol of the man and his myth. By that season he had altered the balance of the game, raising the home run from its relatively modest role into baseball's most dramatic event and a sig-nificant force in determining the outcome of games.**

—*"Babe Ruth,"* Sports Illustrated, *September 1, 1998*

◆ ◆ ◆

H e hit at least six homers against every American League Club that year, though he saved his most stinging punishment, 11 home runs, for his old team, the Red Sox.

—*"Babe Ruth,"* Sports Illustrated, *September 1, 1998*

HIGHLIGHTS

◆ When Ruth hit sixty home runs in 1927, it was more than any other American League team hit that year. He was thirty-two years old. The sixty home runs represented about 14 percent of the league total (439). For that to happen today, a player would have to hit more than three hundred homers a season.

◆ Tom Zachary was the only pitcher who gave up home runs to Babe Ruth while pitching for two different clubs in 1927. On June 16 while pitching for the St. Louis Browns he gave up Number 22; on August 16 as a Washington Senator, Number 36, and on September 30, the sixtieth.

◆ Babe's sixtieth home run was hit in 153rd game of a 154-game season. It was actually game 151 for Babe, as he did not play in two games.

◆ Babe hit fifty-nine home runs in 1921, when he was twenty-six years old. When he hit his sixtieth home run in 1927, he was thirty-two.

◆ As most fans know, when Roger Maris hit 61 home runs in 1961, he played in a season of 162 games. One can speculate on what Ruth would have done with eight more games.

◆ In 1961, Maris had 590 official times at bat; in 1927, Ruth had batted 540 times. It should also be remembered that 1961 was the first year of major league expansion, and thus Maris faced numerous pitchers who just entered the major leagues.

◆ In 1927, the total number of home runs hit in the American League was 533; in 1961, the total number of home runs hit in the American League was 1,534.

◆ In three additional seasons, Ruth hit more than fifty home runs, and altogether he had eleven seasons with better than forty home runs. Except for 1961, Maris's best home-run season was 1962, when he hit thirty-three; in no other year did he hit as many as thirty home runs.

◆ Despite Babe's sixty home runs in 1927, he was not chosen MVP of the American League. He had won the title in 1923 and the rules at that time prohibited any one player from winning the award twice.

BREAKING DOWN THE 60 HOME RUNS

◆ First home runs was hit on April 16 against the Philadelphia Athletics

◆ 41 off right-handed pitchers

◆ 19 off left-handed pitchers

◆ 28 hit at Yankee Stadium

◆ 32 hit on the road

◆ Last 11 were over the right-field fence

◆ 2 were grand slams: September 27 number 57 off Lefty Grove of the Philadelphia Athletics; September 29 number 59 off Paul Hopkins of the Washington Senators

◆ Hit 2 in a single game 8 times

◆ Number 60 was Babe's 299th lifetime home run

◆ The most hit against one team was 11—against the Boston Red Sox

◆ The least was 6 against the Chicago White Sox

◆ Babe's famous number 3 was not on his uniform when he hit his historic 60th home run in 1927. It was in 1929 when the Yankees became the first team to permanently wear large numbers on the back of both their home and away uniforms. The numbers corresponded to the batting order. Ruth was number 3, Lou Gehrig was 4.

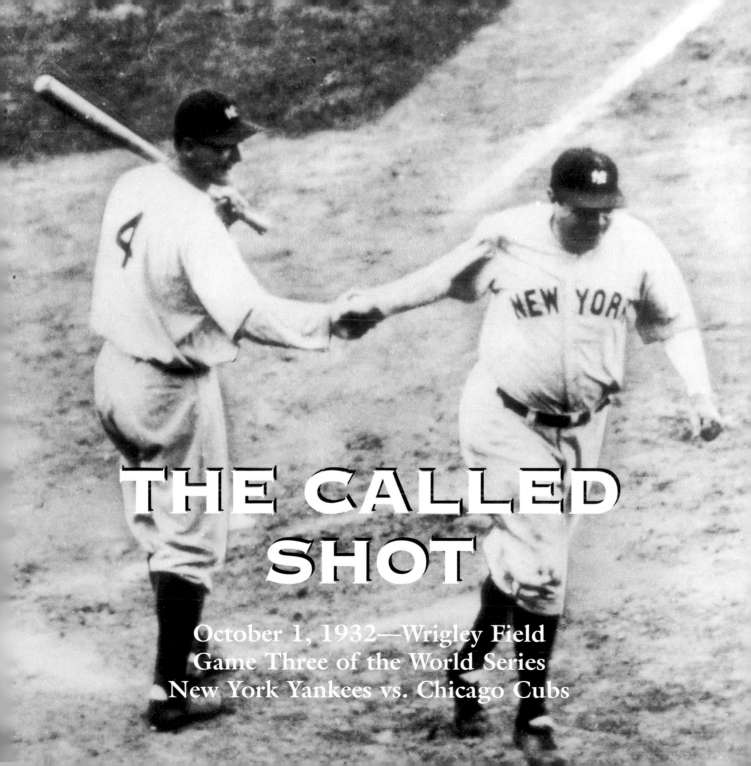

THE CALLED SHOT

October 1, 1932—Wrigley Field
Game Three of the World Series
New York Yankees vs. Chicago Cubs

Babe Ruth did it! In the 1932 World Series between the Yankees and Cubs, Ruth pointed to the center field bleachers, then hit the next pitch, POW, into those bleachers. He hit a change-up curve farther than anybody had ever bashed a baseball at Wrigley Field. You don't believe me? You don't believe Ruth was brash enough, flamboyant enough, foolish enough to call his shot? Believe it!

—STAN HOCHMAN, Philadelphia Daily News, *August 1998*

Babe's pointing to the center field stands indicating where he was going to hit the ball is the most famous and debated gesture in baseball history. His called shot is an episode that is still played out by historians.

At the 1932 World Series in Chicago, as Babe came up to bat in the fifth inning, the Cubs' bench and fans were taunting him unmercifully with a barrage of boos, catcalls, and insults. Babe was now in a counterattack mode and ready for a dramatic showdown.

The called shot was his second home run of the game and the last of his fifteen home runs in World Series play. The Yankees were leading the Series 2–0. Babe's blow was the margin needed for the 7–5 victory.

October 1, 1932, at Wrigley Field

"In the top of the fifth inning the score was tied, 4–4. I was batting in front of Ruth and I led off that inning. I grounded out. Babe stepped up, and just the sight of him was enough to set that place to jumping—the Cub players, the fans, everybody. Charlie Root was the pitcher. The Babe took one strike. Then two strikes. With each pitch the yelling was getting louder and louder. Babe? He was just as calm as he could be. He was enjoying it all, that son of a gun. You couldn't rattle Babe Ruth on a baseball diamond. No, sir!

"After the second strike Babe backed out and picked up some dirt. He rubbed his hands, looking square into the Cub dugout. What was coming out of there was just turning the air blue. He looked at Burleigh Grimes who was cussin' at him, and Babe cussed him right back. Burleigh had a towel around his neck, which he took out and started to wave. Then Babe raised two fingers and pointed to the center field fence. Do I believe he really called it? Yes Sir. I was there; I saw it. I don't care what anybody says. He did it."

—Joe Sewell, *New York Yankee third baseman who batted in front of Ruth, quoted in Donald Honig*, The October Heroes

"I had seen nothing my first time at bat and that came close to looking good to me, and that only made me more determined to do something about taking the wind out of the sails of the Chicago players and their fans. I mean the fans who had spit on Claire (my wife).

"I came up in the fourth inning with Earle Combs on base ahead of me. My ears had been blistered so much before in my baseball career that I though they had lost all feeling. But the blast that was turned on me by Cub players and some of the fans penetrated and cut deep. Some of the fans started throwing vegetables and fruit at me.

"I stepped back out of the box, then stepped in. And while Root was getting ready to throw his first pitch, I pointed to the bleachers which rise out of deep center field.

"Root threw one right across the gut of the plate and I let it go. But before

Lou Gehrig congratulates Babe after his called shot.
Lou hit a homer right after Babe.

the umpire could call it a strike—which it was—I raised my right hand, stuck out one finger and yelled, Strike one!

"The razzing was stepped up a notch.

"Root got set and threw again—another hard one through the middle. And once again I stepped back and held up my right hand and bawled, Strike two! It was.

"You should have heard those fans then. As for the Cub players they came out on the steps of their dugout and really let me have it.

"I guess the smart thing for Charley to have done on his third pitch would have been to waste one.

"But he didn't, and for that I've sometimes thanked God.

"While he was making up his mind to pitch to me I stepped back again and pointed my finger at those bleachers, which only caused the mob to howl that much more at me.

"Root threw me a fastball. If I had let it go, it would have been called a strike. But this was it. I swung from the ground with everything I had and as I hit the ball every muscle in my system, every sense I had told me that I had never hit a better one, that as long as I lived nothing would ever feel as good as this.

"I didn't have to look. But I did. That ball just went on and on and on and hit far up in the center-field bleachers in exactly the spot I had pointed to.

"To me, it was the funniest, proudest moment I had ever had in baseball. I jogged down toward first base, rounded it, looked back at the Cub bench and suddenly go convulsed with laughter.

"You should have seen those Cubs. As Combs said later, 'There they were—all out on the top step and yelling their brains out—and then you connected and they watched it and then fell back as if they were being machine-gunned.'"

—BABE RUTH, *as told to Bob Considine,* The Babe Ruth Story, *1948*

The first man up in this inning will be the mighty Babe Ruth. Babe has already hit a home run with two on—and now, as we look out into the outfield, they're shifting just slightly over into right-center field. And there comes Babe out of the Yankee dugout now, swinging his big club, and the crowd gives him a standing ovation. He seems to be having some kind of an argument with the boys on the Chicago bench. They've been ribbing Babe Ruth all afternoon. They've been warned several times by the umpire to get back there on the bench or he'd chase them to the showers. Now the fans are ribbing Babe as well! Ah, but looking down there at the smiling face of Babe Ruth, he's taking it good-naturedly! And now he doffs his cap in acknowledgment for his first plaudits.

"Babe Ruth steps into the batter's box. Now Charlie Root gets the sign from his catcher, Gabby Hartnett. Here's the first pitch. And it's a strike—right down the middle! And the fans are certainly giving it to Babe Ruth now. Looking over at the Cub's bench, the Cubs are all up on the top step. And they're yelling, 'flatfoot' and throwing liniment and everything else at Babe Ruth! But he steps out of the batter's box. He takes a hitch in his trousers, knocks the dust off his shoes. And now he's back in there again. And Root winds up again and here it comes! And it's outside— and it's evened up on Babe Ruth! Boy what a powerful figure he is at the plate!

"And once again, Root gets the signal, winds up, and here it comes . . . and it's called strike two! And the fans are giving it to him from all corners of this Wrigley Field. The Cubs are up on the bench—they're all hoping that Babe Ruth will strike out. Again, Charlie Root winds up. And here's the pitch—and it's high inside, and it drove Babe Ruth out of the batter's box! And the count is ball two and strike two. And, boy, the Cubs are giving it to Babe now!

"Oh, oh Babe Ruth has stepped out of the batter's box. And he steps about two feet away from home plate. Now he steps toward the Cub's dugout! We thought for a moment that he was going over to toss his bat at them or something! No, he's smiling at them! He takes off his hat, holds up two fingers with his right hand. Now he drops his bat and he's indicating that the count is ball two and strike two. He gets back into the batter's box. The umpire again warns the Cubs! Charlie Root gets his signal. And Babe Ruth steps out of the batter's box again! He's holding up his two and two. Oh, oh, and now Babe Ruth is pointing out to center field and he's yelling at the Cubs that the next pitch over is going into center field! . . . Someone just tossed a lemon down there. Babe Ruth has picked up the lemon and now he tosses it over to the Cubs' bench. He didn't throw anything; he sort of kicked it over there. After he turns, he points again to center field! And here's the pitch . . . It's going! Babe Ruth connects and here it goes! The ball is going, going, going—high into the center-field stands, into the scoreboard! And it's a home run! It's gone! Whoopee! Listen to that crowd!"

—TOM MANNING, *NBC announcer, October 1, 1932, at Wrigley Field in Chicago,*
quoted in Curt Smith, Voices of the Game, *1987*

"No, I didn't point to any spot, but as long as I'd called the first two strikes on myself, I hadda go through with it. It was dammed foolishness, sure, but I just felt like doing it and I felt pretty damn sure Root would put one close enough for me to take a cut at, because I was showin' him up. What the hell, he hadda take a chance as well as I did or walk me?

"How that mob howled. Me? I just laughed."

—BABE RUTH, *commenting on his called shot in the 1932 World Series against the Chicago Cubs,*
third game, fifth inning, score tied 4–4, Yankees ahead in the series 2–0

The act of hitting a baseball often thrown at the blinding speed of 90 to 95 miles per hour has been adjudged the single most difficult task faced by any athletic competitor. Now here was the Babe not only promising to hit the darn thing—but also swearing out an affidavit on it! Chutzpah to the nth degree.

Ruth trotted around the bases triumphantly, his great stomach shaking with laughter. When he reached home plate, Gehrig gripped the Babe's outstretched hand. Beaming, Ruth winked at Lou.

"You do the same thing," he chuckled.

—RAY ROBINSON, Iron Horse: Lou Gehrig in His Time, *1990*

Relics and souvenirs from the called shot series (1932)

With the Cubs riding him unmercifully from the bench, Ruth pointed to center and punched a screaming liner to a spot where no ball had ever been hit before.

—Joe Williams, *New York World-Telegram*

◆　◆　◆

This much is known. There was no love lost between the two clubs. For one thing, new Yankee manager Joe McCarthy had been fired by the Cubs the year before. And Mark Koenig, the longtime Yankee shortstop, had been traded to Chicago in August. Although he hit .353 in 33 games, he was voted only a half-share before the series. That irritated some Yankees.

—Bill Koenig, USA Today Baseball Weekly, *August 12–18, 1998*

145

"Ruth did not point at the fence before he swung. If he'd made a gesture like that, I'd have put one in his ear and knocked him on his ass."

—CHARLIE ROOT, *Chicago Cub pitcher, quoted in Lawrence S. Ritter and Mark Rucker,* The Babe: The Game That Ruth Built, *1997*

◆　◆　◆

I took two strikes and after each one, I held up my finger and said "That's one" and "That's two." That's when I waved to the fence. I just laughed to myself going around the bases and thinking, "You lucky bum."

—BABE RUTH, *quoted in Bill Koenig,* USA Today Baseball Weekly, *August 12–18, 1998*

◆　◆　◆

To this day controversy swirls around baseball's most famous home run. Did he or didn't he? Only Babe Ruth could keep us wondering and arguing for over 60 years.

—ELINOR NAUEN, 100 Years of Baseball, *1999*

1932 NEW YORK YANKEES
WORLD CHAMPIONS

Back row—EDDIE FARRELL, CHARLIE RUFFING, GEORGE PIPGRAS, WILCY MOORE, CHARLIE DEVENS, DANNY MacFAYDEN, ART JORGENS, JOE SEWILL, JOE GLENN
Middle row—CY PERKINS, JOHNNY ALLEN, ED WELLS, TONY LAZZERI, LEFTY GOMEZ, BABE RUTH, WALTER BROWN, LOU GEHRIG, EARLE COMBS, LYN LARY, DOC PAINTER
Front row—HERB PENNOCK, SAM BYRD, FRANK CROSETTI, ART FLETCHER, JOE McCARTHY, JIMMY BURKE, MYRIL HOAG, BEN CHAPMAN, BILL DICKEY
Seated on ground—JIMMY MARR (Mascot)

The World Champions swept the Chicago Cubs 4–0.
Babe is in the second row, sixth from left.

Official World
Series Program
(1932)

BABE
AND THE KIDS

"He probably had more direct influence on the youth of this country than any other ball player during my time. He has created an expectation of hero worship on the part of the youth of this country and it was almost a fortunate thing that Ruth kept faith with the boyhood of America because they loved him."

—BRANCH RICKEY, *general manager, St. Louis Cardinals, 1917–42, and Brooklyn Dodgers, 1942–54, quoted in John Tullius,* I'd Rather Be a Yankee

Babe had a special devotion and adoration for kids, more than any other group of fans. Wherever he went he was besieged by wide-eyed youngsters seeking their hero's autograph. Good-natured Babe always obliged. He gave a lot of himself and was known to stay after games for hours talking to his admirers and signing whatever they put in front of him. No player has ever signed more autographs.

Whether in New York or on the road, Babe frequently visited children in hospitals. He never wanted publicity for it; he just wanted to bring some cheer into their lives. Many people felt that Babe's love for kids was, on some level, a way for him to reclaim the childhood he never had.

Ruth reveled in the smile of a child. In their eyes he saw himself. He enjoyed the innocence and spontaneity of adolescence. Forsaken by his parents, he wanted kids to feel the love and affection he never really had felt.

—Babe Ruth, *HBO Documentary, 1998*

◆　◆　◆

"One child can influence him more than a dozen grown men of affairs."

—FORD C. FRICK, New York Evening Journal, *July 2, 1927,*
quoted in G. H. Fleming, Murderers' Row, *1985*

Babe's love of kids was sincere. In many ways he was a big kid himself. I was in his room for dinner on the eve of the World Series in Chicago in 1932. (He always ate in his room before games because he would have been mobbed by fans and autograph hustlers in the hotel dining room.)

"I've got to go for a short trip, Grant," he said.

"Where are you going right before a World Series?" I asked.

"I'll tell you but if you print it I'll shoot you. I'm going to take a baseball to a sick kid on the other side of town. I promised his mother and father I'd come. He is pretty sick."

The place was 20 or 30 miles away—over an hour to get there and another to get back. No publicity.

—GRANTLAND RICE, *sportswriter and author,* The Tumult and The Shouting, *1954*

152

Babe taking time on a trip to Nova Scotia to pose with local kids

It's easy to see why he is a favorite with the rising generation. He always has time to say "Hello!" to the little lads and to autograph baseballs, score cards, and torn bits of paper. It is sometimes as much as an hour before he can break away from the horde of ragged admirers who waylay him after the game in all the cities on the circuit. Few popular heroes have been as deserving of their popularity as G. H. Ruth.

—JOHN KIERAN, New York Times, *April 26, 1927*

Alice Doubleday Rhodes recalled a time when Ruth played an exhibition game in her small town when she was about ten. For some reason she accepted a dare to get Ruth's autograph, and well before the game she sneaked onto the field and walked to the Yankee bench.

She had to ask, "Which one is Babe Ruth?" and this, to her confusion, made everyone laugh. He was pointed out and when she walked over to him he said, pleasantly enough, "You want to see me, sister?" She handed him her school notebook and a pen, a brand-new pen that had just been given to her for her birthday.

"Here," she said. He signed his name, in a beautiful, even hand and gave her back her schoolbook and pen. "There you are, sister, now don't go home and sell it." But she had promised to get autographs for her schoolmates too. She handed book and pen back to him and said, "Write some more. Write on all the lines." The other players broke up laughing. Ruth shrugged and slowly wrote his name on line after line until the page was filled. "That okay now?" he said, not smiling. He handed her the book and, looking out at the field, absentmindedly put the pen in his own pocket. Her marvelous birthday pen. She did not know what to do. Ruth looked at her coldly, "Something else on your mind, little girl?" he asked. She shook her head and said, "No, sir," and left. Chagrined and not a little afraid, it took her some time to get up the courage to tell her father what had happened, and she was totally unable to understand his hilarity when she did tell him.

"Babe Ruth swiped your pen?" he howled.

—ROBERT W. CREAMER, Babe: The Legend Comes to Life, *1974*

The man was a
boy, simple, artless,
genuine and
unabashed. This
explains his rapport
with children, whom
he met as intellectual
equals. Probably his
natural liking for
people communicated
itself to the public to
help make him an
idol.

—RED SMITH, *author and
columnist*, The Red Smith
Reader, *1982*

Surrounded by his young admirers

"He'd grown up a bad boy and he never wanted any of us to go through what he went through. He used to lecture us along those lines. 'Do what your mother tells you to do and do what your father tells you to do.' If he heard a kid swearing he would yell out at him, 'Goddamn it, stop that goddamn swearing over there!'"

—THOMAS FOLEY, *peanut vendor at Fenway Park in Boston, 1917–19, quoted in* Babe Ruth, *HBO Documentary, 1998*

◆　　◆　　◆

"When I was a boy, I caddied for Ruth out at Wheatley Hills in Long Island. He'd give us a two-dollar tip if he won, and a dollar and a half if he lost. The usual tip was a quarter, or at best a half-dollar. And on the thirteenth hole, where the refreshment stand was, that's where you tested your man. Some golfers would buy you a soft drink, some wouldn't buy you anything. Ruth always said, 'Get whatever you want.'"

—JACK REDDING, *quoted in John Tullius,* I'd Rather Be a Yankee, *1986*

In 1943 he played a round of golf in the rain at the Commonwealth Country Club near Boston. As he was teeing up on the first hole he noticed two boys staring through a chain-link fence.

"Hey," he called to them. "You want to follow me around? It won't be any drier but it'll be more fun. You want to?"

The kids nodded. "Show them how to get into this joint," Ruth said to Russ Hale, the club pro. He waited until the boys reached the tee before he hit his drive, and he walked down the fairway with one arm around each, talking. He played nine holes in the rain, most of the time laughing and joking with the other men in his foursome, but always returning to the kids to make sure they were enjoying themselves.

—ROBERT W. CREAMER, Babe: The Legend Comes to Life, *1974*

Golfing with his friends. Instead of power in the air, a gentle touch on the ground. Babe considered becoming a professional golfer once out of baseball.

It seems that a kid named Billy Kennedy had come all the way from Manchester, N.H., the previous day to watch George do his stuff, and George had failed him. Now, Babe Ruth is no ordinary figure in the life of Billy Kennedy, because the Bambino helped to save his life.

A year ago an automobile whizzed around the corner and into the street where Billy was running out a base hit and beat him to the curb. He was so seriously hurt that the doctors despaired. Four operations were performed, and finally the head surgeon told Billy's father that if the little fellow's strength held out he might pull through.

"If only we can get him to want to live badly enough, he may do it," he said.

That made Billy's father think of Babe, for Babe was Billy's idol. So he sat down and wrote a letter to Mr. Babe Ruth, New York City, enclosing a check and asking for an autographed baseball, "From Babe to Bill."

The ball came right back. So did a telegram, which read: "Tell Billy for me that he must get well and strong and come to Boston to see me play." It was signed Babe Ruth.

Billy was there long before the first game of Tuesday's double header to fulfill his part of the bargain. He wanted to see his hero hit a homer. His hero tried— and didn't.

"Come back tomorrow and I'll hit two to make up for it," Babe promised. This time he didn't fail. He rarely does when something big depends upon him. Quite a fellow, Babe Ruth!

—BILL CORUM, New York Evening Journal, *June 23, 1927*

Visiting St. Ann's orphanage in Tacoma,
Washington, on a barnstorming trip

Having fun with the St. Mary's
Industrial School band

"**A**lmost every weekend Babe Ruth would come in and help us bagging peanuts. He worked for a couple of hours with us. Then he would throw a ten or twenty dollar bill on the table where we were working. 'Take care of the kids.' Then he'd walk out."

—THOMAS FOLEY, *peanut vendor at Fenway Park in Boston, 1917–19, quoted in* Babe Ruth, *HBO Documentary, 1998*

Babe took the St. Mary's band around to Yankee games to help them raise money for the school after it was ravaged by a fire.

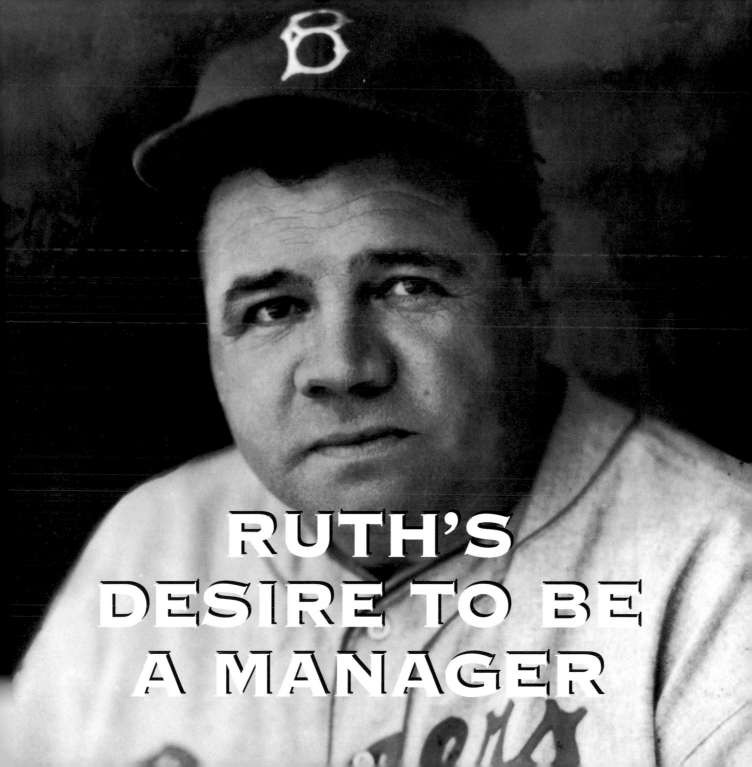

RUTH'S
DESIRE TO BE
A MANAGER

> **"He really did want to manage. I think it was the biggest disappointment of his whole life."**
>
> —Julia Ruth Stevens, *Babe's daughter, in* Outside the Lines:
> Babe Ruth's Larger Than Life Legacy, *ESPN Documentary, 1998*

Babe's one unfulfilled desire was to be a major league manager. As his playing ability declined, he became obsessed with wanting to manage. But the Yankees and baseball turned their back on Babe. Most owners thought that Babe had not been successful at managing himself, therefore, they felt that it was improbable that he could manage others.

Babe was so desperate to find a managerial job that he once offered his services to the Yankees for a dollar a year. He was finally offered a job at managing a Yankee farm team, the Newark Bears, but turned it down, holding out for the big leagues. Years later, he realized that he should have taken the job. Newark was a solid club and if he had been successful, it could have been his entry to the majors.

Babe was deeply disappointed that no team wanted him. His wife, Claire, frequently said that from the day he played his last game until the day he died, Babe sat by the phone waiting for an offer. Sometimes when he could not take it anymore, he would break down, put his head in his hands, and weep.

"I built this
house . . .
I wanted to
be the
manager of the
Yankees and
they wouldn't
let me."

—BABE RUTH, *quoted by
David Blumenthal, in* Outside
the Lines: Babe Ruth's Larger
Than Life Legacy, *ESPN
Documentary, 1998*

Babe with daughter Julia. This
is Julia's favorite picture with
her dad.

"I wanted to stay in baseball more than I ever wanted anything in my life. But in 1935 there was no job for me, and that embittered me. I came to think that the greatest cartoon I had ever seen was one drawn at that time by Burris Jenkins, of the *New York Journal-American,* showing me walking down the road that leads away from the Yankee Stadium. Burris portrayed me in a ragged uniform, fat and elderly. A road marker, reading 'To Oblivion,' or something like that, pointed the way. At my heels snapped a lot of dogs, marked with such signs as 'Ungrateful Owners' and 'Jeering Fans,' and so forth. And in the background was the Yankee Stadium, labeled, 'The House that Ruth Built.'

"I felt completely lost at first. I thought I'd wake up and find it was a bad dream, and when it became apparent that it wasn't a dream I felt certain that the phone would ring and it would be the Yankees or some other big league team in search of me—telling me it was all a mistake. But the phone didn't ring."

—BABE RUTH, *as told to Bob Considine,* The Babe Ruth Story, *1948*

Ruth did have several managing opportunities, but for one reason or another they all fell through. The Detroit Tigers had been interested in him late in 1933, but eventually they had turned to Mickey Cochrane instead. Ruth himself was largely to blame. Frank Navin, owner of the Tigers, asked him to come to Detroit to discuss the matter, but the Babe was on a tight exhibition game schedule and postponed the meeting. By the time Ruth was ready to meet, Navin had decided to hire Cochrane.

Not going to see Navin immediately was "one of the great boners of my career," Ruth wrote in his autobiography.

—LAWRENCE S. RITTER AND MARK RUCKER, The Babe: The Game That Ruth Built, *1997*

◆　　◆　　◆

"So after a while I began staying away from the Stadium and trying to get my mind off my disappointment. I turned to golf and played every possible hour of the day. Without it I would have blown up to 300 pounds. Without it, also, I would have gone nuts."

—BABE RUTH, *as told to Bob Considine,* The Babe Ruth Story, *1948*

◆　　◆　　◆

One thing Ruth had, and one thing which would have helped as a manager had he ever been granted the opportunity, was that he was a grand competitor. That part of Babe's make-up has been stressed surprisingly little in any account of his career, but he was a bear-down guy from away back. He took almost fool hardy chances on fly balls merely because he wanted to win.

—TOM MEANY, Babe Ruth: The Big Moments and the Big Fella, *1947*

In 1938, Ruth returned to baseball as a coach of the Brooklyn Dodgers. He was led to believe they would let him manage some day, but this promise was never kept. The Dodgers wanted him to join the team for his name and to attract fans, not because they wanted him as a manager.

Babe's last major league affiliation was with the Brooklyn Dodgers as a first-base coach.

BABE
ON THE BABE

Although it was his slugging that brought him international fans, Babe was most proud of his 29⅔ consecutive scoreless innings as a Red Sox pitcher in World Series play in 1916 and 1918.

"What I am, what I have, what I am going to leave behind me—all this I owe to the game of baseball, without which I would have come out of St. Mary's Industrial School in Baltimore as a tailor, and a pretty bad one, at that."

—BABE RUTH, *comment made as he watched the making of*
The Babe Ruth Story *in Hollywood, quoted in the* Sporting News
at the time of his death on August 16, 1948

Asked about himself, Babe would always respond with a straightforward answer. While other public figures zealously guarded their privacy, Babe held no secrets and spoke about whatever was on his mind. He was approachable, unpretentious, fun loving, and seemed to perpetuate an ongoing celebration of himself. Here are some of Babe's insights and reflections on his life and career.

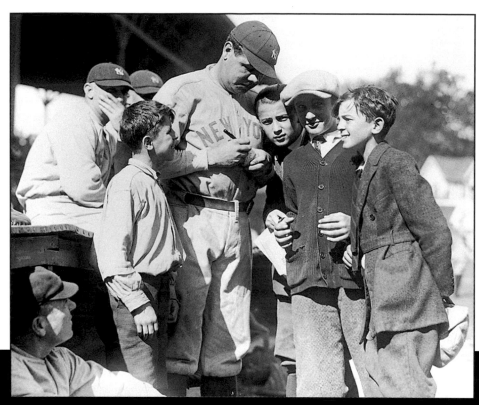

Babe returned to Baltimore in the early 1930s to play an exhibition game and sign autographs for the hometown kids.

"**S**omebody asked me when I was real young what I wanted to be when I grew up. I was so struck by the idea that I instantly put it out of my head. I think because I never wanted to do anything 'cept play ball. I mean I never thought of growing up in the sense that I always wanted to feel the same way I always remembered feeling. Lou Gehrig was quoted as being 'the luckiest guy on earth.' Maybe he hung out with me too much 'cause I consider myself to be the most absurdly fortunate guy to have slid into the 20th century safe."

—BABE RUTH, *quoted in C. Brooke Rothwell's article in* The Best of Spitball, *1988*

"I came up as a southpaw pitcher and pitchers aren't supposed to hit—or to clutter up the batter's box trying to hit during practice. I saw no reason why I shouldn't take my licks. I'd get them, usually, but there were times I'd go to my locker and find my bats sawed in half."

—BABE RUTH, as quoted in Grantland Rice, The Tumult and The Shouting, 1954

◆ ◆ ◆

"Fred Lieb referred to the Yankee Stadium as 'The House That Ruth Built' in the New York Evening Telegram. Other writers liked the phrase, and many still use it today. And I always feel proud when I see it."

—BABE RUTH, as told to Bob Considine, The Babe Ruth Story, 1948

◆ ◆ ◆

He recognized his role as a public entertainer and understood it. In the 1946 World Series the Cardinals made a radical shift in their defense against Ted Williams, packing the right side of the field and leaving the left virtually unprotected.

"They did that to me in the American League one year," Ruth told the columnist Frank Graham.

"I coulda hit .600 that year slicing singles to the left."

"Why didn't you?" Frank asked.

"That wasn't what the fans came out to see."

—RED SMITH, author and columnist, The Red Smith Reader, 1982

Duckpin bowling was invented in 1900 in Baltimore. Babe, a frequent bowler, enjoyed knocking 'em down.

"The reason I supposedly didn't know anybody's name is because they all knew mine."

—BABE RUTH, *quoted in C. Brooke Rothwell's article in* The Best of Spitball, *1988*

"We went out to a hotel for breakfast and while I was studying the menu I heard a player near me say, 'Order anything you want, kid. The club pays our feed bills during spring training.'

"I looked at him, unable to believe it. 'You mean I can eat anything I want, and it won't cost me anything?' I asked him.

"'Sure. Anything.'

"'I was on my third stack of wheat cakes and third order of ham, and hadn't even come up for air, when I realized that some of the other fellows were watching me. I looked at them silently, and kept chewing.'"

—BABE RUTH, *shortly after joining the Baltimore Orioles in 1914, as told to Bob Considine,* The Babe Ruth Story, *1948*

Babe perhaps "calling his shot" in
pool, another favorite pastime

"Those Yankees were the best team. Figure it out. After we got going we won twelve straight World Series games—twelve in a row. It was murder. The Yankees had the greatest punch baseball ever knew. We never even worried five or six runs behind. Ruth-Gehrig-Lazzeri-Combs-Dickey—wham, wham, and wham!—no matter who was pitching."

—BABE RUTH, *quoted in John Tullius,* I'd Rather Be a Yankee, *1986*

"During that 1935 Braves training season I was a big draw. People were curious to see how I looked in a National League uniform, but the harder I tried the worse I did. My old dogs just couldn't take it any longer. It was more and more of an effort to move over the outfield or run down to first base. I had tried hard to condition myself, but it just was torture. I was forty-one and playing my twenty-second season in the big leagues.

"The kids were striking me out or making me pop up on balls I could have hit out of the lot a few years before. It was a rotten feeling."

—BABE RUTH, *as told to Bob Considine,* The Babe Ruth Story, *1948*

"I played just a little too long . . . about a week or so. I should have quit that day in Pittsburgh—I was with the Braves, you know—when I hit three home runs and got gypped out of a fourth one by one of the Waners.

"That should have been curtains. But I had promised old man Fuchs that I'd hang around for his Memorial Day crowd. Too bad . . ."

—BABE RUTH, *quoted by Bob Considine,* Sporting News, *1947*

"It was pretty much of a nightmare. If I had it to do over again, the last 28 games of my 2,503 and my last 6 home runs would never have been entered into the records."

—BABE RUTH, *as told to Bob Considine*, The Babe Ruth Story, *1948*

"The worst of this is I no longer can see my penis when I stand up."

—BABE RUTH, *on gaining weight, as told to Frederick G. Lieb*, Baseball as I Have Known It

For the first two months of the 1935 season, Babe played for the Boston Braves. He retired on June 2, 1935.

"I've heard people say that the trouble with the world is that we haven't enough great leaders. I think we haven't enough great followers. I have stood side by side with great thinkers—surgeons, engineers, economists; men who deserve a great following—and have heard the crowd cheer me instead . . .

"I'm proud of my profession. I like to play baseball. I like fans, too . . . But I think they yelled too loudly for the wrong man . . .

"Most of the people who have really counted in my life were not famous. Nobody ever heard of them—except those who knew and loved them . . . I knew and loved them . . . I knew an old priest once . . . How I envy him. He was not trying to please a crowd. He was merely trying to please his own immortal soul . . . So fame never came to him.

"I am listed as a famous home-runner, yet beside that obscure priest, who was so good and so wise, I never got to first base."

—BABE RUTH, *quoted in "Fame—What I Think of It,"* American *magazine, August 1933*

"The war came along and, indirectly, it brought about my last appearance in uniform in Yankee Stadium. In the summer of 1942, Walter Johnson and I put on an exhibition for the benefit of the Army-Navy Relief. I hadn't had a bat in my hands for four years, and Walter hadn't thrown a ball in that time.

"We went out on the field and it was one of the great thrills of my life in the game. The crowd that day numbered 60,000 and there was a new and lustier note in it—because of the war. It stood on its hind legs and gave us a terrific ovation.

"Walter threw me 21 pitches. On the 21st all the cobwebs seemed to drop off my baseball muscles. I gave it everything I had and hit it up into the third deck in right field, one of the comparatively few balls ever hit up there. That was enough for me. I knew I couldn't top that, so I trotted around the bases and the little show was over.

"They were still yelling for us as we disappeared into the Yankee dugout and started down to the dressing room. We walked along, gabbing and signing autographs, but there was a kind of sadness in both of us. Walter had been the greatest pitcher in the league; I had been the greatest slugger. But he was no longer a part of the game, and the same was true of me."

—BABE RUTH, *as told to Bob Considine*, The Babe Ruth Story, *1948*

"This was the
first time I met
Babe Ruth and
I was speechless.
I was twenty-two
years old."

—Yogi Berra, *April 2000*

Babe, after he retired, with a
young Yogi Berra circa 1947

BABE'S
FINAL YEARS

> **"When I think of death I think of the ballpark of God's imagination. I'll be hitting 'em out where ever I go."**
>
> —BABE RUTH, *quoted in C. Brooke Rothwell's article in* The Best of Spitball, *1988*

After being traded to the Boston Braves for the 1935 season, Babe played for two months before he decided to call it quits. By his own admission, he did not have the physical and mental edge that he had always required of himself.

But it would have been uncharacteristic of Babe to exit baseball without a tremendous game for the record books. On May 25, he walloped three consecutive home runs in Pittsburgh—the second time in his career he hit three in one game during the regular season. Babe's last thundering blast, Number 714, traveled over six-hundred feet and was the only home run to ever sail over the roof in Forbes Field. This was also his last hit.

Babe played his final game in Philadelphia at the Baker Bowl on May 30, and retired on June 2. Now forty years old, he went on doing what he had done before—being Babe Ruth. He occupied his time playing golf, bowling, and listening to popular radio shows. One thing is for sure: Babe never faded from the spotlight, and often used his celebrity status to help raise money for charitable causes.

In 1946, Babe was stricken with a rare cancer, naso-pharyngeal, and underwent an operation that reduced his voice to a raspy whisper. For a long time his family and doctors were able to keep the seriousness of the illness from him, but he gradually grew weaker and weaker. Babe succumbed to his illness on August 16, 1948, at age fifty-three. It was heartbreaking to see this indomitable man waste away.

The spotlight always followed Babe wherever he went, even toward the end of his life.

America's No. 1 convalescent, Babe Ruth, received his first visitor the other day and told him how to hit a home run. The visitor was Hank Greenberg, who called their visit unforgettable—as indeed it was.

The greatest home-run hitter who ever lived, and the best there is in baseball today, met in Ruth's trophy-littered apartment. I was there to listen.

Greenberg was like a boy sitting at the feet of the stricken master. He asked for, and got, Babe's autograph.

"Going to tell you something, Hank," Babe husked in a voice that is just returning to him after his critical neck operation. "Hand me that bat. Now I'm going to show you the whole secret of how I hit those home runs. Only fellow I ever told it to was Lou Gehrig, when Lou first came up to the Yanks and Miller Huggins was trying to make a left-field hitter out of him."

Ruth wrapped his huge and now gaunt hands around the bat handle, with the little finger of his right hand extending down below the main surface of the handle and butt.

"Look," he said, as he sat in his robe and pajamas and lightly swung the bat. "See how this grip makes your wrists break at the right moment? Throw the whole weight of the bat into the ball. With this grip, you've just got to follow through. Any other grip interferes with your follow-through.

"I kept it a secret a long, long time," Babe mused.

—BOB CONSIDINE, Sporting News, *1947*

"No man ever got letters like those. Before I left the hospital there were 30,000 of them. Most of them were written in the penciled scrawl of kids, and telling me that I was going to get well. Most of these boys had never seen me play; in fact some of them had not been born when I stopped playing. But they seemed to look upon me as a friend in need of comfort—and I was.

"I insisted that every letter be answered. The actual job of writing replies was attended to by Cary Lowenstein, and my good friend May Singhi Breen, the radio star. But I signed them. In fact that's the one thing I'll never give to any person—the right to sign my name for me."

—BABE RUTH, *as told to Bob Considine,* The Babe Ruth Story, *1948*

In recent years, there have been various attempts to strip away the legend of Babe Ruth, but there is no way to do this, for even after you strip away, you are left with the legend. Almost all the responsible things said about the man were true, the good and the bad, so the legend strippers usually settle by pointing out that the Babe liked women and drinking, which separates him from most healthy young men, and sometimes behaves badly, which sets him apart from humanity. And what is left is the Swash Buckler who shaped the course of baseball and much else in modern sports, who set records that lasted for decades. In other words, a legend intact.

—JOHN MOSEDALE, The Greatest of All

Ruth was terribly bitter when I went to visit him in 1947, when he had cancer and was on his way out. He wouldn't have anything to do with anybody, he wouldn't do any interviews. I was just lucky that he was willing to see me. At that point he was very disappointed by the way he had been treated. It's true that he was a hero for some twenty years, and patted on the back and spoiled and applauded, but that's the way it goes. You're going to get that adulation from a fickle fan, but the owners should have appreciated what he contributed to the game and made an effort to ease him out of baseball with a little more dignity.

—HANK GREENBERG, *Detroit Tiger first baseman, 1930, 1933–41,*
The Story of My Life, *1989*

BABE RUTH DAY

Babe Ruth Day was one of the first simulcast broadcasts linked by radio. The Babe was very ill and had been in Florida but returned to New York for this event.

A. B. (Happy) Chandler, the commissioner of baseball, declared that Sunday, April 27th, 1947, would be Babe Ruth Day in the major leagues. Ceremonies were held in all the ball parks, but the most significant one was in Yankee Stadium. Ruth returned to New York in time to be at the Stadium for his day. Almost 60,000 people were in the Stadium. Ruth spoke too, bending forward slightly from the hips to bring his mouth close to the microphone. His speech was extemporaneous, and his voice was raspy and low.

"Thank you very much, ladies and gentlemen. You know how bad my voice sounds. Well, it feels just as bad. You know, this baseball game of ours comes up from the youth. That means the boys. And after you've been a boy, and grow up to know how to play ball, then you come to the boys you see representing themselves today in our national pastime. The only real game in the world, I think, is baseball. As a rule, some people think if you give them a football or a baseball or something like that, naturally, they're athletes right away. But you can't do that in baseball. You've got to start from way down, at the bottom, when you're six or seven years old. You can't wait until you're fifteen or sixteen. You've got to let it grow up with you, and if you're successful and you try hard enough, you're bound to come out on top, just like these boys have come to the top now.

"There's been so many lovely things said about me, I'm glad I had the opportunity to thank everybody. Thank you."

He smiled and waved to the crowd and walked slowly to the Yankee dugout.

—ROBERT W. CREAMER, Babe: The Legend Comes to Life, *1974*

In the Yankee locker room on June 13, 1948, Babe's last appearance at Yankee Stadium

His Last Visit to Yankee Stadium

On his last visit to Yankee Stadium, "the house that Babe built," the Yankees retired Babe's number 3.

On Sunday, June 13, 1948, the Yankees celebrated the twenty-fifth anniversary of Yankee Stadium, and Ruth was invited to be there along with other members of the 1923 Yankees. Sick as he was, he was delighted with the idea.

All the other old-timers had been introduced, the applause from the big crowd rising and falling as each name was called. It was time for Ruth. He got to his feet, letting the topcoat fall from his shoulders, and took a bat to use as a cane.

He walked slowly, and he was smaller than Babe Ruth should have been. He paused for the photographers, leaning on the bat, looking up at the crowded tiers of people. At the microphone Ruth spoke briefly, saying how proud he was to have hit the first home run in the Stadium and how good it was to see his old teammates. Ruth left the field at Yankee Stadium for the last time.

—ROBERT W. CREAMER, The Babe: The Legend Comes to Life, *1974*

Celebrating the twenty-fifth anniversary of Yankee Stadium, June 13, 1948. Babe's number 3 was retired. Legendary Yankee announcer Mel Allen is standing near Babe.

THE DEATH OF BABE

It rained that day. Even the heavens wept at the passing of Babe Ruth.

—ARTHUR DALEY, *sportswriter,* New York Times, *1920s to 1950s*

◆ ◆ ◆

When he died, Ruth was accorded a tribute worthy of a world leader. His body lay in state from 5 P.M. August 17 until 7 A.M. August 18 inside the main entrance of Yankee Stadium. He was dressed in a double-breasted blue suit and clutched a set of rosary beads in his left hand. More than 100,000 fans waited in line for hours to file past his body.

—BILL KOENIG, *"Frail from Cancer, Ruth Was Last to Know He Was Dying,"*
USA Today Baseball Weekly, *August 1998*

The motorcade carrying Babe's casket approaching St. Patrick's Cathedral in New York on August 19, 1948

"Babe Ruth is dead. The Sultan of Swat, the man who was Mister Baseball to every kid in America, was buried yesterday in New York. While his bat is forever stilled, while the memory of his boyish grin will fade with the generation, the mighty Bambino will not be forgotten as long as baseball endures. On sandlots and in stadiums wherever there is the crack of a bat meeting a ball, or the roar of the crowd at a play well done, there will be George Herman Ruth, idol of millions, a sportsman on and off the field. Although there were dark clouds in his life, the Babe never had much use for sadness. Nor would he want us to be sad. I ask that everyone arise for a few seconds in final tribute to Babe Ruth."

—A. B. (HAPPY) CHANDLER, *commissioner of baseball, August 20, 1948, before a crowd of 100,000 at a football game in Chicago*

The crowd arrived early, a throng so long it spilled out of Yankee Stadium and onto the adjacent streets. The people lined up side by side, four and five abreast winding around the ballpark. For two days the mourners filed by his coffin, a steady stream that began early in the morning and stretched until midnight. When it had ended 77,000 people had come to say farewell to an American hero, a baseball player lying in state like a president, in the ballpark he defined.

—HAL BOCH, Associated Press, *August 19, 1948*

There was an outpouring of emotion at Ruth's funeral. As he lay in state at Yankee Stadium and people passed his coffin, the Yankee equipment manager, Pete Sheey, cried as he mopped the stone floor. He had remembered that the Babe had taken up a collection for the clubhouse staff back in the days before they were cut into World Series shares.

Ruth is buried at the Gate of Heaven Cemetery in Hawthorne, New York—approximately one hour north of New York City in Westchester County, not far from the Tappan Zee Bridge.

Babe's funeral procession leaving St. Patrick's

A half century after Ruth's death, fans still come and leave stuff by his grave. A half century from now, that scene and the legend of Babe Ruth will be no different.

—STAN HOCHMAN, Philadelphia Daily News, *August 1998*

IN THE COMPANY
OF BABE

Chatting with his teammate Lou Gehrig

Here are some of the more prominent records Babe set and the players who went on to surpass his benchmarks. Some records still stand. Statistics of active players to date as of publication.

YANKEE STADIUM, NEW YORK, NEW YORK, OCTOBER 1, 1961

By victimizing pitcher Tracy Stallard, Roger Maris exorcised a ghost. In 1927, Babe Ruth hit sixty home runs in a 154-game schedule; in 1961, the Rajah unloaded his sixty-first in Game No. 163. After a frenetic season, his pursuit of the Babe marred by angst and cacophony, for Maris, a golden time. "If I never hit another home run," he said, "this is one they can never take away from me." He hit 117 more home runs; they never did.

—CURT SMITH, Voices of the Game, *1987*

ATLANTA-FULTON COUNTY STADIUM, ATLANTA, GEORGIA, APRIL 8, 1974

At 9:07 P.M., in his second time at bat, in the Braves' first home game, Henry Aaron—of whom Stan Musial said, "He thinks there's nothing he can't hit."—lofted a fly ball toward the sullen Georgia sky. When the ball descended, it cleared the fence, and Aaron had eclipsed a hero, breaking the unbreakable: the career home-run record (714) of the Sultan of Swat.

—CURT SMITH, Voices of the Game, *1987*

Babe's Benchmarks

Bases on Balls	2,062	Career Singles	1,517
At-Bats	8,399	Career Doubles	506
Hits	2,873	Career Triples	136
Runs Scored	2,174	Career Home Runs	714
Lifetime Average	.342	Steals	123
Home Run Average	11.8	Stole Home	10
Slugging Percentage	.690	Caught Stealing	118
Multi-Homer Games	72	Total Bases	7,972
Home Run Titles	12	Major League Games	2,503
RBI Titles	6	Minor League Games	46
Slugging Titles	13		

MULTI–HOME RUN GAMES

Babe Ruth	72	Harmon Killebrew	46
Mark McGwire*	64	Mickey Mantle	46
Willie Mays	63	Willie McCovey	44
Hank Aaron	62	Mike Schmidt	44
Jimmie Foxx	55	Barry Bonds*	43
Frank Robinson	54	Lou Gherig	43
Eddie Mathews	49	Dave Kingman	43
Mel Ott	49	*Still Active	

LIFETIME RECORDS

BASES ON BALLS

Record set by Babe in 1935

Babe Ruth	2,062
Ted Williams	2,019
Rickey Henderson*	2,009
Joe Morgan	1,865
Carl Yastrzemski	1,844
Mickey Mantle	1,734
Mel Ott	1,708
Eddie Yost	1,614
Darrell Evans	1,605
Stan Musial	1,599
Pete Rose	1,566
Harmon Killebrew	1,559
Lou Gehrig	1,510

*Still Active

RUNS SCORED

Ty Cobb	2,245
Babe Ruth	2,174
Hank Aaron	2,174
Pete Rose	2,165
Rickey Henderson*	2,135
Willie Mays	2,062
Stan Musial	1,949
Lou Gehrig	1,888
Tris Speaker	1,882
Mel Ott	1,859
Frank Robinson	1,829
Eddie Collins	1,821
Carl Yastrzemski	1,816

*Still Active

MOST CAREER HOME RUNS

Record set by Babe Ruth in 1935 at 714

Hank Aaron	755
Babe Ruth	714
Willie Mays	660
Frank Robinson	586
Harmon Killebrew	573
Reggie Jackson	563
Mike Schmidt	548
Mark McGwire*	545
Mickey Mantle	536
Jimmie Foxx	534

SLUGGING AVERAGE

Total bases divided by at-bats

Babe Ruth	.690
Ted Williams	.634
Lou Gehrig	.632
Jimmie Foxx	.609
Hank Greenberg	.605
Joe DiMaggio	.579
Mark McGwire*	.579
Larry Walker	.579
Rogers Hornsby	.577
Albert Belle*	.573
Frank Thomas	.573

AVERAGE HOME RUNS PER AT-BAT

Mark McGwire*	10.8
Babe Ruth	11.8
Ralph Kiner	14.1
Harmon Killebrew	14.2
Juan Gonzalez	14.2

MOST RUNS BATTED IN

Hank Aaron	2,297
Babe Ruth	2,213
Lou Gehrig	1,995
Ty Cobb	1,960
Stan Musial	1,951
Jimmie Foxx	1,921
Eddie Murray	1,917
Willie Mays	1,903
Mel Ott	1,861
Carl Yastrzemski	1,844

*Still Active

SINGLE-SEASON RECORDS

MOST RUNS SCORED IN A SINGLE SEASON

Record set by Babe in 1921

Babe Ruth	177	1921
Lou Gehrig	167	1936
Lou Gehrig	163	1931
Babe Ruth	163	1928
Chuck Klein	158	1955
Babe Ruth	158	1920
Babe Ruth	158	1927
Rickey Henderson*	146	1985

MOST HOMERS IN CONSECUTIVE SEASONS

Mark McGwire*	128	1997–98
Mark McGwire*	128	1998–99
Sammy Sosa*	127	1998–99
Babe Ruth	114	1927–28
Babe Ruth	113	1920–21
Ken Griffey, Jr.*	112	1997–98

*Still Active

50 HOME RUNS, 150 RUNS BATTED IN, 400 BASES IN A SINGLE SEASON

	Team	Year	HR	RBI	TB
Babe Ruth	Yankees	1921	59	171	457
Babe Ruth	Yankees	1927	60	164	417
Hack Wilson	Cubs	1930	56	190	423
Jimmie Foxx	Athletics	1932	58	169	438
Sammy Sosa*	Cubs	1998	66	157	410

OVER 50 HOME RUNS IN ONE SEASON

Babe Ruth	4
Mark McGwire*	4
Jimmie Foxx	2
Ralph Kiner	2
Willie Mays	2
Mickey Mantle	2
Ken Griffey, Jr.*	2
Sammy Sosa*	2

*Still Active

FEWEST GAMES TO 60 HOME RUNS

Mark McGwire*	142	1998
Sammy Sosa*	148	1999
Sammy Sosa*	149	1998
Babe Ruth	154	1927
Roger Maris	159	1961

MOST HOME RUNS IN A SEASON

Mark McGwire*	70	1998
Mark McGwire*	66	1999
Sammy Sosa*	66	1998
Sammy Sosa*	63	1999
Roger Maris	61	1961
Babe Ruth	60	1927
Babe Ruth	59	1921
Jimmie Foxx	58	1932
Hank Greenberg	58	1938

*Still Active

ALL-TIME WORLD SERIES LEADERS—BABE SET THE RECORDS

MOST RUNS SCORED

Mickey Mantle	42
Yogi Berra	41
Babe Ruth	37
Lou Gehrig	30
Joe DiMaggio	27
Roger Maris	26

MOST HOME RUNS

Mickey Mantle	18
Babe Ruth	15
Yogi Berra	12
Duke Snider	11
Lou Gehrig	10
Reggie Jackson	10

HIGHEST SLUGGING AVERAGE

Reggie Jackson	.755
Babe Ruth	.744
Lou Gehrig	.731
Lenny Dykstra	.700
Al Simmons	.658
Lou Brock	.655

MOST TIMES STRUCK OUT

Mickey Mantle	54
Elston Howard	37
Duke Snider	33
Babe Ruth	30
Gil McDougald	29
Moose Skowron	26

Most Hits

Yogi Berra	71
Mickey Mantle	59
Frankie Frisch	58
Joe DiMaggio	54
Hank Bauer	46
Pee Wee Reese	46
Gil McDougald	45
Phil Rizzuto	45
Lou Gehrig	43
Eddie Collins	42
Elston Howard	42
Babe Ruth	42

RBI

Micky Mantle	40
Yogi Berra	39
Lou Gehrig	35
Babe Ruth	33
Joe DiMaggio	30
Bill Skowron	29
Duke Snider	26
Hank Bauer	24
Bill Dickey	24
Reggie Jackson	24
Gil McDougald	24

Most Games

Yogi Berra	75
Mickey Mantle	65
Elston Howard	54
Hank Bauer	53
Gil McDougald	53
Phil Rizzuto	52
Joe DiMaggio	51
Frankie Frisch	50
Pee Wee Reese	44
Roger Maris	41
Babe Ruth	41

500 CLUB

Ranked by the number of at-bats it took to reach the 500th homer

	At-Bats	Games	AB/HR	Career Home Runs
Mark McGwire*	5,487	1,639	10.97	545
Babe Ruth	5,801	1,740	11.60	714
Harmon Killebrew	6,671	1,955	13.34	573
Jimmie Foxx	7,074	1,971	14.15	534
Mickey Mantle	7,300	2,316	14.60	536
Mike Schmidt	7,331	2,118	14.66	548
Ted Williams	7,454	2,210	14.91	521
Willie Mays	7,533	1,987	15.07	660
Willie McCovey	7,582	2,377	15.16	521
Eddie Mathews	8,280	2,291	16.56	512
Frank Robinson	8,427	2,318	16.85	586
Reggie Jackson	8,599	2,417	17.20	563
Hank Aaron	8,612	2,204	17.22	755
Ernie Banks	9,204	2,442	18.41	512
Mel Ott	9,273	2,660	18.55	511
Eddie Murray	11,095	2,950	22.19	504

*Still Active

THE FEWEST AT-BATS TO 500 HOMERS

Mark McGwire	5,487
Babe Ruth	5,801
Harmon Killebrew	6,671

MOST NO. 1 AND TOP-FIVE FINISHES IN SINGLE-SEASON STATISTICS SINCE 1900

Hitters No. 1		Hitters Top Five	
Babe Ruth	70	Ty Cobb	122
Ty Cobb	63	Stan Musial	111
Ted Williams	61	Honus Wagner	106
Rogers Hornsby	58	Lou Gehrig	105
Stan Musial	51	Babe Ruth	105
Honus Wagner	46	Ted Williams	101
Mike Schmidt	35	Hank Aaron	100
Hank Aaron	31	Willie Mays	95
Lou Gehrig	31	Rogers Hornsby	94
Willie Mays	30	Mel Ott	90

—STEVE NADEL, *USA Today Baseball Weekly*

Other Facts

◆ On August 5, 1921, a baseball game was broadcast for the first time in Pittsburgh at Forbes Field. Harold Arlin called the play-by-play on station KDKA, as the Pirates defeated the Philadelphia Phillies 8–5.

◆ In 1921, the Yankees won their first pennant but lost to the New York Giants in the World Series. It was the same scenario in 1922. In 1923, the Yankees won their first World Series. Babe had three home runs in the Series, beating the Giants four games to two. The Yankees hit .293 as a team and Ruth hit .368 with three home runs, eight walks, and eight runs. It was the first million-dollar Series, the first gate of 300,000, and the first broadcast of a Series.

◆ Babe never played a game at night. May 24, 1935, was the first night game in major league history. The Philadelphia Phillies played the Cincinnati Reds.

◆ The first American League night game was May 16, 1939. The Cleveland Indians played the Philadelphia Athletics.

◆ In 1969 Babe was voted the Greatest Baseball Player of All-Time by the Baseball Writers Association of America in celebration of the Centennial Year of Baseball.

Always identified
with baseball,
Babe remains a part
of every season.
It all goes back to
"The Babe."

Oh, make no mistake. The Babe is still here. Still out in the land, his shadow enveloping his sport as well as his country in a way nobody—in any profession—has ever been able to duplicate. He is still the most memorable man who ever wore a uniform. He is Babe Ruth, the greatest of all time.

—MIKE BARNICLE, ESPN the Magazine, *September 14, 1999*

211